ONCE MORE
AROUND
JERICHO

"I give my enthusiastic support to Dr. Ralph Winter, whom I have known, admired, and held in high esteem for more than thirty years. He is a man of vision, dedicated to our Lord, with unusual ability. I am confident that the Center for World Mission, which he heads and for which he has ambitious plans, will become a reality and will encourage all who are concerned about giving a helping hand to World Missions."
---*Bill Bright*

"I don't know of any other organization or institution in the world which is uniquely going to do what the Center for World Mission proposes to do."
---*Leighton Ford*

"I heartily endorse and support the United States Center for World Mission. Let's join hands together and make this a success for the advancement of the Kingdom of God throughout the world."
---*Billy Graham*

"The U.S. Center for World Mission is probably the single most strategic institution and movement in the world today aimed at evangelizing the two billion persons who can only be reached by cross-cultural, "missionary" evangelism."   ---*Donald Hoke*

"Your vision is cosmic in its breathtaking dimension. It is a Biblical response both to an obvious need as well as to the clarion call of the scriptures to finish the work of world evangelization. Who cannot but hope and pray that God through the influence of His people will not make this vision a reality."
---*Harold Lindsell*

"I cannot recall any Christian organization only $2\frac{1}{2}$ years old that has gained such widespread support and the confidence of leaders from all over this country. This is unique in our time."
---*Donald McGavran*

ONCE MORE AROUND JERICHO

THE STORY OF
THE U.S. CENTER
FOR WORLD MISSION

Second edition July 1976-July 1979

Roberta H.
Winter

For super busy people, see
the overview on page 238

William Carey Library

1705 N. SIERRA BONITA AVE • PASADENA, CALIFORNIA 91104

Library of Congress Catalog Card Number 78-66367
International Standard Book Number 0-87808-167-4

Second Edition

Published by the William Carey Library
1705 N. Sierra Bonita Avenue
Pasadena, California 91104
Telephone (213) 798-0819

To Tricia

CONTENTS

FOREWORD

It may sound funny, coming from me, to say that I am surprised and excited by this book. I knew my wife, Roberta, was working away at it, but I didn't pay much attention. She didn't ask me any questions. It was completed before I saw a page of the manuscript.

When I finally sat down to read it, I was really impressed. I could never in the world have captured as she does the moods and moments of the stranger-than-fiction true account she relives so lightly and yet so passionately. But this is not just an exciting story, inviting you to be a spectator. It is a gauntlet thrown down, we believe, from Heaven: God is asking sincere, believing Christians in America to stop in their tracks and to re-evaluate the way of life to which they have gradually become accustomed in the last twenty years.

Our garages are bulging with things we may have never really needed. Our schedules are bulging with nice things that do not dramatically help the world's helpless. Our menus are bulging with food that makes us overweight. Our bookstores are bulging with books on the abundant life ... for *us* in *America*. Our churches are bulging with Americans who have been drinking in blessings for years. (Some say that 80% of all the trained Christian workers in the world are in America.) We are vaguely proud of our past achievements in missions.

But today new, hard questions are being asked. Today it is suddenly clear that we are not well enough aware of what has been done in missions to be suitably impressed by either the amazing successes of the past or the amazing scope of the unfinished task in the future.

When our people talk these days about missions at all, the first subject that often arises is the delightful possibility that the new Christians overseas can finish the job by themselves. Well, all right! The presence of the overseas church, this "new fact of our time," must be taken into account.

Yet, if there is any validity to the vision this book describes, it is the awesome fact that a large number of the world's non-Christians — about five out of six — live in communities or social strata within which there is no culturally relevant church from which evangelistic outreach can be made, unless in fact outreach to these people is "missionary" outreach which crosses the barriers that departmentalize such people. This presents a disturbing limitation to what any church, anywhere, can do. Neither at home are the home churches effectively reaching through such barriers, nor are the overseas churches effectively reaching through such barriers. It is as though the number of missionaries in the world working in new fields has suddenly shrunk, instead of being increased by virtue of the help of the overseas church.

I spell this out in some detail because the massive concern and effort and excitement which my wife describes is utterly senseless apart from this single amazing insight. Everything else flows from there.

Perhaps you too will be caught up in the flow. Don't resist. This book is talking about the highest of all priorities.

Ralph D. Winter

PREFACE

Writing this, my first book, has been quite a spiritual experience for me. There were times when I despaired of ever being able to get on paper what I felt in my heart. It was not easy in all the bustle going on at the U.S. Center for World Mission even to find a quiet spot where I could think, and for some weeks I wrote in a corner of the storage room.

But now it is finished, even though the story is not. God has been very gracious to all of us here, and especially to me as I wrote. Over a year ago Ralph asked several to keep diaries so we could look back on what God had done. But all too often those diaries were sketchy, and I had to depend on my own memory.

In deliberating about the one to whom I would like to dedicate this volume, I thought of a number of people who have assisted me throughout. Mercedes Gribble is one of these. She has been with us through this entire period of time, and carefully went over my manuscript, making valuable suggestions here and there. I thought of our wonderful staff at the Center, and especially of Mrs. Prudence Dancy who has been like a dear younger sister and yet so spiritually mature. I thought of my husband, without whose encouragement I could not even have had the time allotted to this task. I considered our four beautiful daughters — Beth, Becky, Linda and Tricia, all of whom have unselfishly participated with us in this challenge. I finally decided that of all those I might choose, I owe the most to Tricia. She was in her last two years of high school while all these events took place. During the summer she worked (and sang and prayed) with us every day, but during the school year she has missed much of what has happened. She needed a mother's presence at home, especially these last two years before she leaves for college, and I often arrived late from the office, feeling guilty that she was alone so much. But God has blessed this daughter in particular with grace — a grace which manifests itself in unselfishness, understanding compassion, a natural wisdom beyond her years and the ability to smile from the heart when she receives far less than she deserves. She loves the Lord dearly, and all of us love her dearly. It is to her that I dedicate this book.

1

JULY 1974
"LET THE EARTH HEAR HIS VOICE"

I leaned forward in my chair, trying to catch some of the words of the language spoken by the girl with the long blond braids seated in front of me.

"Maybe she's Swedish," I thought, "or Norwegian." All around me people were listening over the earphones, as the message being given from the platform was, at the same time, being translated into French, German, Spanish, Chinese, and Japanese, their native languages. The girl and her companions were all dressed in black. There were two women — herself, and one older; the rest of the group were men. The young girl was obviously their interpreter.

"Finland, Hungary, Yugoslavia, Austria?" My mind kept clicking off all the European countries from which a blond girl so dressed could have come.

There was a pause in the meeting as the speaker on the platform sat down, and I leaned forward and tapped the girl on the shoulder. "Excuse me, would you tell me something? What country do you and your friends come from?"

"We're from Rumania," she answered.

"Rumania! Oh, I'm so glad you came," and I sank back in my chair. Even from behind the Iron Curtain, then, they had come. And we were all here to worship the same Christ and to discuss together the task of worldwide evangelization. As I looked about this room with the multiplicity of earphones, the bank of translation booths off to one side, and the colorful assortment of national costumes visible everywhere, it was clear to me that the gospel could not have reached so far without surmounting a jungle of language barriers. Yet I wondered if anyone would believe my husband when he told them, come Saturday, that most of the language and culture barriers were *still* to be crossed!

My husband, one of the Congress speakers, had been asked to deal with precisely that subject — cross-cultural evangelism. He called it "the highest priority."

We were seated in the big hall at Lausanne, Switzerland, there for Billy Graham's International Congress on World Evangelization. Two thousand, seven hundred participants from all over the world were there, and many had brought their wives. The great convention hall was crowded. From the back rows those on the platform seemed almost toy figures moving about. High above the speaker's head a large screen depicted on closed circuit television every gesture and facial expression of the one speaking.

Ralph knew many of the people, so many, it seemed to me, that out in the central lobby we couldn't walk more than five steps before he was greeting or being greeted by someone. Some were friends, mission executives or evangelical leaders from other parts of the United States. Others were his former students — missionaries and national leaders from India, Africa, Taiwan, Australia, Germany, Latin America and Singapore. By now he had had more than a thousand in his classes at the School of World Mission of Fuller Theological Seminary.

Ralph was to give the plenary address* on Saturday morning. We knew from the flurry of responses which had already come to us from his pre-congress article that this address would be controversial. All the people here were in some way involved in evangelism, but most of them were evangelizing their own people — people of their same culture and language. Ralph wanted to show that Christians everywhere must engage in evangelizing across cultural barriers — the remaining missionary task.

"We are able to evangelize our own countries," a few of the Christians from India and Africa had written in their pre-conference responses. "The day of the missionary is past. We don't need missionaries any more."

Ralph applauded their desire to get involved themselves in evangelizing their own people, "but," he insisted as he gave his address, "the job remaining to all of us is not only immense, it is still mainly beyond all present outreach. There are 500 million people still to be won in India, 600 million Muslims, 800 million Chinese, 100 million tribal peoples, as well as many others scattered around the world. Yet, even supposing every church in the world reached outside its doors and won everyone within range — people who spoke the same language and came from the same culture — do you realize that even then only one out of six of the non-Christians in the world would be evangelized?"

The figures were too staggering. Most did not quite understand. Ralph's words were like a time bomb that had not yet gone off. Yet I knew that his data was accurate, as accurate as anyone's could possibly be. I had been with him through the years when he was amassing those statistics. He had drawn on the most reliable sources, and he did graduate work in statistical calculations. Yet I also knew that many at that congress would find it hard to believe there was so much yet to be done — *beyond new barriers!*

"We're spending all our time in evangelizing," some had insisted, prior to the congress.

"Yes, I know that is true, and that is wonderful. But whom are you evangelizing? If you are like most evangelists, pastors and missionaries, almost all your efforts are spent bringing nominal Christians to a real and vibrant relationship with Jesus Christ. And even when your church does win people from a totally non-Christian background, are these not almost entirely from within your own cultural group? Who will win those people who are beyond?"

The words were not comfortable to hear. But were true. I glanced around me to see if the audience truly understood. They were listening intently, with apparent understanding and increasing conviction. "Nominal Christians need to be truly saved," Ralph was saying, "and I'm all for the kind of evangelism that brings such people into a personal relationship to Christ. But if we are seeking the *largest, most difficult* evangelistic task still remaining to be done, it is *not* winning these nominal Christians nor even winning non-Christians who speak our various languages and are from our same cultures. We cannot forget these people. We must reach out to them even more than we have in the past — yet if we are speaking of the evangelistic task that must have highest priority today, we must refer to those who have never had a chance to hear the gospel in their own language and cultural setting. Of 2.8 billion non-Christians in the world, these number 2.4 billion, over half the population of the world. Despite all the wonderful mission work across the years and the outreach of national churches everywhere, there are still *2.4 billion people beyond the present efforts of any existing church or mission.*

5

I could hear the intake of breath from someone behind me — he was astonished, incredulous, unbelieving. On the platform, his face televised on the screen high above him, Ralph put it more vividly. "If everyone of us had stopped on our way to this Congress and won *a million people* to Christ, we could have disbanded this congress. The job would have been done. Each delegate here would have had to win *one million people*. That is the size of our unfinished task."

Would we respond to that need?

That message at Lausanne was for the participants, but God also meant it for Ralph. Was his role only to be that of a "voice crying in the wilderness" pointing the way? Or was he also to set an example, personally?

That was the lesson which almost two years later launched us on the greatest adventure of our lives.

---

*This address was printed in *Let The Earth Hear His Voice,* edited by J. D. Douglas and available in many Christian bookstores. It was published by World Wide Publications, 1313 Hennin Avenue, Minneapolis, Minn. 55403. This address was also printed by permission by the William Carey Library both in *Crucial Dimensions of World Evangelization* and as a separate pamphlet entitled "The New Macedonia: a Revolutionary New Era Begins."

2

SEPTEMBER 1974 - MARCH 1975
THROUGH THE VALLEY OF
THE SHADOW
(Psalm 23:4)

We were back home in Pasadena. From the crowded halls at Lausanne, Switzerland, we had gone by train and ferry to England, visiting a couple of European missionary headquarters on the way. I had talked until I was hoarse selling books on missions that second week in Lausanne, and had picked up a terrible cold on the train while sitting at an open window to escape the smoke strangling the atmosphere. All this time, by doctor's orders, I had been taking large amounts of thyroid in an effort to reduce two nodules on my thyroid gland which he had discovered just before we left. Now he recommended surgery.

I looked forward to the "rest" that surgery would involve, yet somehow I felt reluctant and ill at ease with the whole idea. "You, a nurse, afraid, and it isn't even major surgery!" I chided myself. Still uneasiness lingered, and I recommitted my life and future to the Lord.

At first the surgery seemed uneventful. The nodules were benign, for which I praised the Lord. The doctor didn't seem too alarmed that I could only whisper — that could be due to the rather large metal tube the anesthetist had placed in my throat. But the surgeon began to be concerned when my voicelessness persisted three days, a week, two weeks, three weeks. And I was getting desperate.

It was the beginning of the seminary school year, and as usual, faculty and students were invited to an opening banquet. I went with Ralph and quite by accident (or providence) sat beside a seminary friend who had recently had problems with his voice. He advised me to see his specialist, whom I called the next day.

I was well, perfectly capable of driving the 45 miles to the doctor's office in Santa Monica. And though I couldn't speak, I could whisper. So I went, alone. I didn't know whether to be impressed or dismayed by the showy display of autographed photos of movie stars which covered Dr. Hans von Leden's walls. Were they a status symbol for him, or was he really a capable laryngologist, I wondered.

As a nurse I knew his exam was thorough. But I was totally unprepared for his diagnosis.

"You either have a bruised or pinched nerve, in which case your voice will soon return, or the surgeon accidentally cut your laryngeal nerve. Your right vocal chord is paralyzed."

"If it is cut, will it grow back together?" I should have known better, yet the alternative was too unthinkable.

"If it is cut there are two options. If we get it before three weeks are out, we can sometimes splice it together. It is too late for that. Sometimes, very rarely, in three out of one hundred cases, the left vocal chord alone will compensate for the right. If this happens to you, your voice will return suddenly after about six months. But don't expect that. It happens very rarely. There is nothing we can do. Nothing but wait."

I was stunned as the truth dawned on me. I might never be able to speak again. I might always have to clap my hands to attract attention, or touch the grocery clerk on the arm, or pull my husband over to my lips as we travelled the freeway. Tears filled my eyes there in the doctor's office as I choked out a whispered, "We can pray." I was fairly sure this man was not a Christian — in fact he was probably Jewish — but I couldn't restrain myself. "There is a greater Physician who made me and can heal me. I will go to Him."

I stumbled out of the office and down the stairs, hoping I would meet no one who would wonder at the tears raining down my cheeks. The long drive home during rush hour traffic was a nightmare. I couldn't see well because of the tears and I worried about the safety of driving in my condition. Yet I had to go home. God's angels must have been very close to me that day.

For some time I had been praying that the Lord would make the Bible more precious to me. I had read the Bible all my life, but sensed that it didn't seem so precious to me as it did to some others who had newly come to it later in life. Disciplined obedience on my part was necessary, I knew, and thus had reread parts of the Old and New Testament. For some time, I had tended to shy away from the prophetic books since their interpretation was, I thought, subject to so much speculation, but of late I had been impressed that obedience required reading these books also. I had completed Daniel and Revelation and now was halfway through the Book of Ezekiel where I had left my marker that morning.

It was a relief to find myself alone when I got home. I wanted to tell Ralph, but not yet. I had a battle to fight with God. Throwing myself on the bed, I cried and prayed and then reached out for my Bible and, for lack of any other idea, started to read where I had left off. And the words leapt from the page as if God himself were speaking, "On the day of his coming your voice will suddenly return to you" (Ezekiel 24:27).

"Oh, God, could this be for me? Dare I claim it?" I searched feverishly for the context — did it mean (for me) when Christ would return? Whose coming? Suddenly! That's what the doctor had said . . . if my voice were to come back it would come back *suddenly!* "Oh God, you must mean this for me. Otherwise why would I see it when I wasn't hunting for it? When I didn't even know such a verse existed?" And my heart became calm and trustful again.

The next months were "toughies." Various pastors and friends prayed for me, but I could sense they didn't really believe God would heal me. Even those who specialized in praying for the sick wanted to warn me against all possibilities, "You know, your verse says, 'On the day of His coming.'" I knew they meant well, and I knew that true faith was not a conjured-up feeling that God would somehow honor. Mine at times was strong. I would assure people that whatever was God's will was OK. I knew I was in His very loving hands. Yet on the way home from such a public declaration I would break down in tears at how long it seemed and how difficult to be patient.

God gave me those months because I needed them. I couldn't rush out and manage this or that because I couldn't make myself heard. Little by little I began to understand the rock of security that the Bible was meant to be, and mine became underlined throughout in pinks, yellows, and greens of felt-tip markers. Every morning I hopefully tried my voice to see if this were my *"suddenly"* day, and every day I again cried to the Lord, reminding Him of His promise, yet assuring Him that I'd serve Him no matter what

— He'd just have to show me how. I constantly prayed that no matter what happened, my attitude would be a testimony for Him and that I would not be resentful of the surgeon who should have been more careful. I wanted especially for the non-Christian doctors to know of God's power — that He is real!

By the end of January, I began to notice a slight difference. The left side of my throat would be very weary at times, and I would stretch my neck to relieve the tension. Then the whisper began to get a bit louder and crack into a real voice for a moment. Day by day there was a bit more voice until in about three weeks I was talking again. How I praised the Lord! Even the Jewish doctor said, "Well, I guess God has done a miracle for you. Your right vocal chord is still paralyzed, but you'll get along OK."

As I look back now, I see that God had me, and our whole family, in training, making us ready to trust Him wholly. If we had been able to do something, anything, we would have done it. But there was absolutely nothing we could do except wait and trust and pray. That lesson was invaluable. We learned that God looks over the daily affairs of man, that He cares what happens, even to us, and that to Him our growing stronger in faith is far more valuable than anything else.

Not my voice, nor our financial security, nor our position, nor anything was to be compared to the value of learning to depend on Him. I needed that lesson for what was to come.

3

THE TWENTY-FIVE
UNBELIEVABLE YEARS

My love for Ralph had grown tremendously during the months of testing before we were married. I had recognized his ability, enjoyed his conversation, and rested in his companionship. With the birth of each of our four daughters I marvelled at his tender, understanding concern and his insistence on staying with me throughout the process. Now I rejoiced. His rocklike undergirding had sustained me daily in a trial that went on for six months.

We had become acquainted almost by chance in 1951, just as I was graduating from nurses' training. Ralph had come to speak at the chapel which the few Christian student nurses organized. In spite of very different backgrounds and the pitfalls of courtship by mail, we were married in five months.

Ralph was different from al¹ others I had dated. He talked about the world and about strange people in strange places. He spoke of dreams, goals for the future, unfinished tasks. He had a way about him of seeing sides to issues that I never imagined existed, and I was fascinated. And he revealed traits of his personality that he knew might scare me off immediately.

"I have a reputation for being somewhat a 'son of thunder,'" he said on our second date. I remembered the reference to James and John but couldn't quite imagine Ralph wanting to call down fire on an unrepentant village, and waited for an explanation.

"I guess what I mean is, when I'm convinced of something, I go all out. Some accuse me of being sort of a fanatic," and he paused. Still I waited. "One summer," he want on, "my mother was terribly embarrassed when I finally concluded I should no longer wear dress clothes, not even to church. I felt it was somehow wrong to spend money on such things when people elsewhere in the world were starving. I still feel that way, but now I see that if the message the church people get from such action is only that you're weird, you've lost the point. So now I wear dress clothes like everyone else, but only as a uniform. I still don't believe it's right to spend a lot of money on them. And I guess that this fundamental willingness to be different, to do things that others may not understand, is very much a part of me. I don't know if I'll ever change there. And I guess most girls would find it difficult therefore to marry a guy like me."

He looked at me somewhat quizzically.

I had other questions: "What are you going to do with your life?" I was impressed that he was beginning studies for a Ph.D. in linguistics and anthropology, but beyond that? "Are you going to be a teacher, an engineer (he had an engineering degree from Caltech), a pastor (he had attended seminary two years)?" And I threw out *my* challenge which had often stopped a relationship in its tracks, "I'm going to be a missionary!"

I watched for his reaction. "I really don't know what the Lord wants of me. John Wesley said 'The field is the world. God has no geographical boundaries.' I know I'm ready to do anything God asks me to do, but I don't know what that is. People keep insisting that I make up my mind. But I'm waiting for God to show me, and doing what seems best in the meantime."

We had only one month to get to know each other before he went back East for graduate studies. I was willing to drift along in our relationship, but he plunged into a thorough research. He talked to a mutual friend about me; he checked out my theology, my reputation, my Christian commitment, my scholastic ability. He even gave me oral math quizzes as we sped along the freeway, which I promptly flunked, every one.

I also was learning many things about him. A mutual friend, also in nurses' training, obviously admired him, yet admitted that his unusual and unexpected conclusions sometimes irritated people. "He is an innovator," she said, "sometimes far ahead of others in his thinking." His actions were also innovative, I found out. He told me of the experimental class in Biblical Greek which he had taught at a Nazarene College, the one I had attended just a few years before. He told me of the program he had initiated which eventually sent many Christian teachers of English to Afghanistan (then and still a country closed to missions). He told me of his boxes of file cards of the Greek vocabulary of the New Testament to be used for producing a series of reference tools for seminary students and Biblical scholars.[2] And I noticed even his conversation was unusual, at times brutally honest, at others extremely diplomatic.

We were married that December, just after Christmas, and three days later flew to New York State. It was in many respects a cross-cultural marriage. I had grown up an Arminian in theology (Nazarene); he a Calvinist (Presbyterian and Congregational). What to me were unintentional "mistakes" were to him, nevertheless, "sins," intentioned or not, if they were contrary to the (known or unknown) will of God. I had to learn to sing Presbyterian hymns instead of Nazarene gospel songs. Being in the East for the first time in my life I had to wear a hat and gloves to church. Even the English spoken there was different; one night in the middle of the night when I woke him to tell him something important he responded with a local colloquialism which set us both off into peals of laughter. It was a period of adjustment, but we were together and we loved each other and knew the Lord had brought us together.

After Ralph graduated from Cornell, we went to Princeton Seminary where he accepted a student pastorate in a little, historic country church. There our two older daughters were born. Up to this time I had gone to class with Ralph, done research for his doctoral dissertation and studied one summer at the Summer Institute of Linguistics while he taught. Now, suddenly, I was housebound, with two lovable but very confining babies. I wanted the babies and I wanted to study, and it seemed I couldn't do both.

Fortunately, for me, Ralph was also frustrated. With a Ph.D. in linguistics he didn't expect trouble in that area. Yet his first week in Hebrew class was his last. "I just can't take it," he complained to me. "The way the Biblical languages are analyzed and taught is simply not up to date. It's a sin! No wonder pastors-to-be learn to hate Greek and Hebrew and rarely ever use them again. But they are required courses. How can I ever sit in that class for a whole year?"

Typically, he started looking for other academic options and found that he could study Hebrew on his own. If at the end of a year he could pass the comprehensive exam in Hebrew, he could skip the regular class. That year he faced a demanding schedule. Besides going to school full time and pastoring a church, he worked every Saturday to supplement our meager income. Hebrew was totally forgotten until six weeks before the comprehensive was to be given, and then Ralph began to panic. I volunteered, "If only I didn't have the babies, I could study with you," (How I would enjoy that! I had studied French and German with him for his doctoral exams, and I knew he hated studying a language by himself.) Thus for six weeks his parents paid for someone to take care of our two babies while we studied Hebrew next door in the church office. That exposure to Hebrew enabled me later to help with his second-year Hebrew homework for his Hebrew exegesis class while I fed our youngest at 2:00 AM. Later I worked on a *Contextual Lexicon of Genesis* which he coauthored with Dr. Charles Fritch, one of the Hebrew professors at Princeton. I enjoyed the mental stimulation again, even though house work suffered.

I enjoyed even more the sense of "partnership" with Ralph in his tasks. To me "helpmate" has always implied helping wherever needed — at home, in the office, in research. And during that period I needed that sense of working *with* Ralph, not just *for* him.

In 1956 we went as missionaries of the United Presbyterian Church to work with highland Indians in western Guatemala. We were fortunate to be assigned to work with an older couple who had a great love and understanding of the Indian culture and saw the missionary task as all-encompassing. They had pioneered the work among 250,000 Indians, being joined much later by several couples in another mission three or four hours away, and by a single nurse who ran the clinic they had started.

Our work during those years involved us in the Theological Education by Extension movement (now spread worldwide), a nationwide rural adult education program offering a government sixth-grade diploma, the formation of the first (and only) junior high school in our town, the establishment of several small industries (tent-making ministries for Indians in seminary), the formation of a credit union, and the establishment of an English-speaking school for both Guatemalans and Americans. Although he delved deep into educational and developmental programs, Ralph was still convinced that the only real answer to man's need was the change of his heart by the Holy Spirit and his incorporation into a continuing body of believers, the Church. By comparison, all other approaches were incomplete and essentially impermanent by themselves. An article to that effect caught the interest of a man who would loom large in our future, Donald McGavran.

Toward the end of our second five years in Guatemala, largely because of his effort in the TEE movement, Ralph was named the Executive Secretary of the Association of Theological Schools in Northern Latin America, and in that capacity became personally acquainted with the seventeen nations north of the equator. When we went back to Pasadena on our furlough in

1966, Dr. McGavran of the newly established School of World Mission at Fuller Theological Seminary asked Ralph to teach a course on Theological Education by Extension. It was a heady experience to work with Dr. McGavran. We had known of him for some time through his writings and had admired his insight and courage in trying out new ideas in mission strategy. Now Ralph had the rare privilege of working at his side and learning from him directly.

We had finally agreed to teach in Pasadena six months a year, and were preparing to return to our work in Guatemala when in a brief space of time Dr. McGavran twice came close to death. He was past the age at which most men retire, but was so energetic that he seemed indestructible. The entire permanent missions faculty at that point consisted of Dr. McGavran and Dr. Alan Tippett, a well-known and capable missionary anthropologist, now retired. Dr. McGavran insisted that Ralph stay the full year and at first we vacillated, trying to know the will of the Lord.

We stayed at Fuller for ten years. Ralph became a full Professor of the Historical Development of the Christian Movement as well as lecturer in Theological Education by Extension and various strategy and statistics courses. To him this was ten years of learning about all parts of the world in the present and in the past. God has truly done marvelous things, starting with that little band of twelve apostles!

But there were gaps. So many things still needed to be done to get the gospel to all the world.

When Ralph had gone from a degree in engineering to anthropology and linguistics, people asked why he had left engineering. They always seemed a bit confused by his answer: "I didn't; now I'm a social engineer!" Then when he went to seminary after getting his Ph.D. in linguistics, his answer to such questions became, "I'm a Christian social engineer." People would laugh. "What on earth is that?" they'd ask, and he would explain, "It's a person who looks for the gaps in the social structure of the Christian cause and tries to fill them."

In a very real sense this has been Ralph's chief calling. If a system of theological education were needed that would train real leaders where they were without tearing them from their jobs and families, then a Christian social engineer should design such a plan. He and another missionary engineer-turned-anthropologist, Jim Emery, did just that. TEE was the result.

If a publishing house specializing in low-cost, high quality books on mission strategy were needed, as the faculty at the School of World Mission believed, then a Christian social engineer should design one that could operate in the black and get its publications to missionaries all over the world. The William Carey Library came into being.

If students making decisions at the Inter-Varsity Missionary Conference at Urbana needed a missions educational program which would help them ascertain God's call for their lives and at the same time give them transferable university credit, then a Christian social engineer should design such a program, fully accredited even in secular universities and spiritually challenging. SIIS (the Summer Institute of International Studies) was born.

More than a professor or a missionary, Ralph is really a Christian social engineer. If to John Wesley "the field is the world," to Ralph "the task is as big as the need, whatever that is." His assignment was teaching and research, and he did that faithfully, curtailing outside speaking engagements far more often than the other professors realized, lest his teaching suffer. And I worked alongside him, doing research for his classes, helping prepare lessons, grading papers and helping him in his writing. But of what value is the planning of strategy if the bridge collapses for want of a span? Of what value is teaching if the cause of which one speaks is weakened for want of a missing link?

I looked forward to weekends, hoping for times to relax. But weekends were filled with engineering projects — Christian social engineering: first the formation of the William Carey Library publishing house and its sister Church Growth Book Club, then the formation of the American Society of Missiology and the development of its journal, *Missiology: An International Review*. Later, after the Urbana Student

Missionary Conference in 1973, came the establishment of the Summer Institute of International Studies. Sometimes I felt that such engineering was as much *fun* to Ralph as a football game was to others. He worked hard on his own time, and he loved it.

These projects, once set up and running, could be turned over to others to operate. But the dream for a U.S. Center for World Mission was big and risky and no one else stepped forward. And it couldn't be done on weekends and after hours. There was no way around it. He would have to leave a job he loved or pass by an amazing challenge. And here we faltered, for seven long months.

---

[1]This chapter title comes from a book by the same name written by my husband and published by the William Carey Library, 1705 N. Sierra Bonita, Pasadena, CA 91104. It discusses the advance in missions between 1945 and 1970. A condensed version appears as the last chapter in Kenneth Scott Latourette's seven-volume *A History of the Expansion of Christianity,* published by Harper and Row.

[2]Two of these tools are coming off the press this summer: *The Word Study New Testament* and *The Word Study Concordance,* companion volumes usable by both laymen and pastors. They will be available from the William Carey Library, 1705 Sierra Bonita, Pasadena, CA 91105, and from Tyndale House.

4

MAY 19, 1976
"IS THERE ANYTHING TOO HARD FOR ME?"
(Jeremiah 32:27b)

"If you need a million dollars, or two, forget it! You'll never raise it. But if you need ten million, then I think you can do it!"

Dale Kietzman, the one speaking, was a member of an organization which specializes in helping Christian organizations develop good management and raise funds. He ought to know. "Anything less just won't attract attention; it is not enough of a challenge. People respond to big challenges."

Ralph was astounded. Being involved from time to time in budget planning in mission circles, he had not become accustomed to thinking in terms of millions of dollars.

The six other men in the room laughed. Millions! He had to be kidding!

"And you can do it without tapping any of the seminary's sources of money," Dale added.

There was a real need for a center, sort of an implementing annex, to carry forward some of the strategies suggested by the missions faculty. All the men admitted that. Just a few months previously the seminary had lost its bid to purchase one of the best missions libraries in existence in the world, even though the world's largest graduate school for missionary research was part of the Pasadena complex. For two years the faculty had dreamed of an associated center (neither legally related to nor funded by the seminary) which could house such a library, as well as many different service mission organizations, editorial offices for missionary journals, and host missions conferences. In short, they wanted it to be a nationwide catalyst for renewal in missions.

Now these men were discussing the use of an entire college campus available in Pasadena.

Was that plan ever to be?

5

JULY 1976
"IF YOU BELIEVE . . .
IT'S YOURS"
(Mark 12:24)

"Hal-le-*lu*-jah!"

Most of the graduating seminary students merely accepted their diplomas, shook hands with the president and the chairman of the board and went back to their seats. But Erik Stadell, from Sweden and a missionary to Greenland, turned to the audience, raised his diploma high and shouted, "Hal-le-lu-jah!"

Everyone laughed. Everyone loved Erik. His faith was vibrantly enthusiastic and he loved his Lord. But in day-to-day matters, it was difficult to take him very seriously. He was too mystical, too unrealistic.

We also wondered what to think about him. Tall and gangly with a Pinocchio nose and a puckish smile, he seemed the opposite of the dedicated scholar, the competent mission leader. His English was adequate, but obviously "different." His mannerisms seemed overly animated, unrealistically enthusiastic — "different" in a lovable way. But, as we came to find out, Erik was far more than what he seemed. For several years he had felt burdened to pray that the Lord would send more laborers into His harvest. With his wife, Erik had had an exciting time in Greenland, working among the Eskimos. But he prayed that God would give him 25 more missionaries to send, not just to Greenland but around the globe. At times he wondered if this idea was from God, or only a dream.

Ralph had been the faculty mentor for Erik's master's dissertation, and Erik was delighted when Ralph encouraged him to write of that dream and the practical way in which God might accomplish it. Could he set up a new Swedish mission board? How would he work out the legal papers? How could he attract and train candidates? Erik got busy on the practicalities called for in such a project.

Now it was July 1976, and he had his first contingent of candidates ready to begin their training in Pasadena, and he asked Ralph to come and speak to them.

I was a bit bemused as I sat in the lounge of the former girls' dorm on the Pasadena College campus where those Swedish students were housed. Did Erik have what it took to start a mission board? He seemed so much a dreamer. But when that meeting began I saw an Erik I hadn't known existed. This man had charisma; he was dynamic, forceful — a tremendous leader! The young people from Sweden all responded to him with obvious deference; they believed in him; they trusted him to hear from God and to lead them.

Erik had his own dreams, and they were large. But at one point his and ours converged.

Two years before, he had come with his family to Pasadena, led all the way from Greenland to a school he hadn't even known existed. Housing was found for him in one of the vacant houses bordering the Pasadena Nazarene College campus. The college had recently purchased a new campus in San Diego, and workmen were busily moving furniture, disassembling offices, and vacating the premises. Erik noticed the activity and started asking questions. He had been praying for some time that the Lord would provide property somewhere which would be utilized solely for world missions, "perhaps even for a new world mission organization." And here was a 17½-acre campus, vacant. Could this be God's answer to his prayer?

About the same time Ralph and the School of World Mission faculty had begun to realize the need for a mission center of some sort. Their dream was not less huge, and it too seemed impossible.

Some years earlier, Pasadena College had built a small prayer chapel at the heart of the campus. As Erik dreamed, he began circling the campus in prayer claiming it for the cause of missions. One day a workman, also a Christian, saw him standing praying by the prayer chapel, and asked him if he would like to pray inside.

"I went in and a burden of prayer came over me. I prayed all day and into the night. My wife sent my children looking for me, but I told them I couldn't leave — not yet. I prayed there for a week before the Lord would let me leave," he told us almost four years later.

Before moving, the college had a sure offer to purchase by a group which wanted to start a Christian college. Now that the Nazarenes were gone, this offer fell through. Others made bids, over 100 organizations in all, but something always happened to prevent the sale. Meanwhile, Erik was praying that somehow the Lord would hold this campus for missions.

August 10, 1975, was a blistering hot day, as most days in August are in Pasadena. Erik and his family had been invited to spend a few days at a friend's cottage on the beach at San Clemente, and this seemed the perfect day to go. They all looked forward eagerly to the swim in the cool ocean. Neither Greenland nor Sweden had prepared them for this climate.

Erik watched his family race to the beach, but felt somehow he couldn't follow them, not yet. He still had something to settle with God. His diary of prayer for that day records that the Lord impressed him with this verse: "Thou shalt speak and say before the Lord thy God,"

(Deuteronomy 26:5). And he went on to claim the campus in Pasadena: "Before the face of the Lord our God we both speak and confess that the campus of Pasadena College is consecrated for world missions and can never belong to any other purpose."

He told us that immediately peace settled over his soul. He dashed to the water and frolicked joyously with his family.

There were other times and other prayers about that campus and Erik wrote in his thesis:

"Never before in my life have I experienced that a prayer *must* become a reality as the prayer that (the) Pasadena College campus will be used for the purpose of world mission. In the name of Jesus Christ, I know that this miracle is pre-destined by God Himself. Written at Pasadena College, Wednesday, December 10, 1975."

The preceding summer the Lord had begun, quite independently, to lay this same burden on Ralph.

6

AUGUST 1976
DREAMS

The faculty of which Ralph was a part was scattered to the winds. The dean was at a conference in South Africa, the former dean in India, one faculty member in Illinois, another in Nigeria. I had often complained that Ralph was usually gone most summers on one trip or another, speaking or teaching here and there. But for some reason or other, Ralph was home during part of July and August that year. And the Lord was talking to him.

That evening when he spoke to the Swedish students was not the first time he had thought of the Pasadena College campus as a world mission center. He had even discussed it with his faculty friends the previous January, but only he seemed excited by the possibilities.

"It costs too much."

"It's too far from the seminary."

"Maybe the administration won't approve."

Erik had walked over the campus with us that evening. We were impressed by the number of large buildings, quite well kept. Surely if God were to give us this campus it would be one of those "abundantly above all that we ask or think" answers to prayer.

In those next few days, Ralph began contacting college officials, one by one, trying to find out the terms of purchase. The college board of trustees had had many offers yet seemed eager to hear him out, even arranging for him to meet the Executive Council at once. They knew we had no money. How could they be interested in us?

"The Lord must have sent you," he was told by one board member. "We are at an impasse. We must sell. We need the money desperately to pay for our new campus. Yet the only good offer we have right now besides yours is from a cult known as the Church Universal and Triumphant or Summit Lighthouse University, and the whole church in the area is up in arms about it. Either we split the church or we split the board."

We began negotiations.

I remembered Gideon and his fleeces. Ralph laid before the Lord some impossible requirements. Only if God somehow made the college board accept those demands could we go forward. The board already had in its hands an unsigned contract with Summit. Would it deal with us instead? We could only pray.

The problems weren't all with the college. It was becoming more and more clear that we would have to step out in faith alone, without the emotional support of many of our oldest friends. Some of the faculty, as they returned one by one from summer trips, were cool to any suggestion that here was the opportunity the faculty had sought. When Ralph was more explicit, stating that he would have to leave the faculty to test whether God was truly behind this dream, there was a very awkward silence. What he was suggesting was not only *not* on the agenda for discussion, it was not to be even considered. At that point only one was willing to state that this dream could be a part of God's plan, and that if so, God would surely complete it. Another compassionately appealed to his church's mission committee for financial support for us, since we would be leaving without salary of any sort. Yet it was some time before any fellow professor visited us on the campus or encouraged us in our new venture. That sense of being very alone in this project was part of the price we had to pay.

Were we ready?

7

SEPTEMBER 1976
NO TURNING BACK

It was past midnight when we left the restaurant. Ralph's hand gripped mine tightly as he said, "Well, Roberta, I guess we've crossed the Rubicon. There's no turning back now."

It had been a quietly determined, but tense, two hours. We had struggled for months with an issue we were asking a superior to understand in minutes. And we sensed he was disappointed. His questions implied that he felt somewhat betrayed, abandoned in midstream. And we were the culprits.

It was the first week of the fall semester. All the professors and students were back on campus. The registration lines at last were dwindling, the orientation introductions and programs complete, and the student body picture taken. During the past few months Ralph had talked several times with various people about what

God was saying to him. Nevertheless when he came to his final decision, it was like jumping off a cliff.

Fortunately Ralph was on sabbatical from teaching, and resigning at this point would create a minimal disturbance. His earliest scheduled class was three months away and he offered to teach his main courses then. He made it clear that even though he was not at all convinced this project would succeed, he was overwhelmingly convinced that God wanted the attempt made. There were hundreds of millions of people beyond the range of any existing church or mission — this he knew. This his research had made very clear. The School of World Mission at the seminary was doing a great thing in helping missionaries on furlough to reach more effectively those with whom they were now working. But the completely unreached people — the "hidden people" — were rarely on the agenda of studies. The problems of the occupied mission fields seemed big enough without asking for even greater ones further beyond.

The decision had been difficult to make. As a full professor in a prestigious seminary, Ralph had professional standing and was often asked to serve in important ways around the world. He had contributed a great deal to mission thinking. Would all his talents now be buried in fund raising? He also had the financial security we needed with two of our four daughters still in college and another about to finish high school.

One had just married, and I knew those expenses were not far off for the other three.

Now we were turning our backs on both honor and security. Our salary would stop, not at the end of the sabbatical as we had hoped, but immediately. We might become the laughing-stock of all who knew us. And some would accuse us of egomania, "Who do you think you are . . .?" Even to contemplate such a step was painful. No school wants a failure on its faculty — especially one who has very publicly tried and failed. We were not so foolish as to hope otherwise. There would be no way back.

I worried about the finances. Could God take care of us? Yes, I knew He *could*. But *would* He? How could I be sure?

Was it God who was leading and not just our own foolish dreams? That was the question I had to ponder. (Ralph had already settled it for himself.) If I could be sure God was guiding this way, then I could trust Him to take care of us.

One day in prayer I felt God tell me, "I will take care of you as well as you have ever been cared for. You will not lack anything you need."

My heart at last was at rest. With the words "When God guides He provides" on my lips and with my hand in Ralph's, I stepped forth into the greatest adventure of my life.

8

OCTOBER 1976
"IF YOU ASK ANYTHING
IN MY NAME"
(John 14:12)

Ralph, his secretary, Prudence, and I stood in the entrance way and looked at "our building."

The previous month the Church Universal and Triumphant (also known as Summit Lighthouse International) had moved onto the main portion of the campus. Erik Stadell and his twenty Swedish missionary candidates had been very discouraged when told they had to move out of the dormitory they occupied to make room for Summit. They were even more discouraged when they came to know more about the group who had rented all but three of the buildings on campus. Summit is an Eastern mystical group who, according to large newspaper articles, revered Bhudda, Krishna, "ascended masters" and practiced chanting and meditation. We had heard that they were very well-behaved, nicely dressed and basically Hindu in religious philosophy, though Americans. The newspapers spoke openly of Summit's intention to buy the campus.

Hundreds of Nazarenes in the area were convinced, however, that this campus was still to be used to bring men to a saving knowledge of Jesus Christ. Erik's little band, after long days and nights of continual prayer, were also convinced that somehow God had special plans for this place. Our own guidance, up to this point completely separate from theirs, seemed amazingly to "fit."

For almost a month Ralph had been talking with college officials about the possibility of our buying the campus as a center for world mission. He had insisted that in order to raise the funds necessary to buy, we had to be physically on the campus somewhere, and the college officials had offered us space in the only building across the street from the main part of the campus. Erik's group were already housed in that building — formerly a dormitory.

We had several additional requests. We needed office space not only for ourselves but for a number of other organizations that wanted to move in with us. We needed to know that members of our team could rent college housing without having to wait long months for a house to become vacant, even though there were over a hundred names on the waiting lists. We needed very generous terms of rental since we could not
 huge monthly sums and raise money to buy

the campus at the same time. Our starting balance, after all, was zero. The college board must be willing to wait a year for the down payment. We would not buy even then if any more of the 84 off-campus houses belonging to the college were sold; yet we could not give the college any money to hold them for us for at least two years.

Ralph had met the week previous with the trustees and lawyer, discussing the conditions essential to us which we knew, humanly speaking, were unreasonable. Yet they had been our fleece, as it were. We felt that if the Lord truly were in this call, if He *truly* wanted us to "go into this land and possess it," He could persuade the college officials to meet these "unreasonable" demands. He did!

Now we stood in the front hall — wide, spacious — and walked into the rooms we were granted for use as offices.

We had asked for 4,000 square feet at a low rental rate plus potential access to the buildings on campus not now occupied by the cult, paying only for space we actually occupied. The college would not rent it to anyone else without asking us. We would have first chance.

Moreover, we could have similar first refusal rights on the rental of any of the 84 houses owned by the college, so that we could literally point to any house now occupied and say, "We want that," and we would have it. In comparison to Ralph's office at the seminary, this one was big enough for a skating rink. Ralph's faith was big, but I wondered to myself if we would ever fill all that space.

Months before when the faculty members had shared a dream, they had discussed a building which would serve all mission societies. It would need to include a large missions library, a graphic arts division to help them with posters and interpretive literature, a film and photography division, a mailing list management office, a research division, and a department which could help with financial planning. Besides supplying these practical needs such a center would also have departments focusing on literacy and translation, health training and community development, and especially on research in evangelistic techniques to win the largest blocs of unreached peoples: the Muslims, the Hindus, the Chinese, and the tribal peoples. The faculty had dreamed of special research centers, too big and specialized for any one mission or any one seminary to inaugurate, but helpful to all missions.

How the word got around that we had space to rent, I shall never know, but various mission organizations began calling Ralph. "Could I rent some office space?" each would ask. Some needed so much space Ralph had to turn them away. Others didn't quite fit the necessary qualification of serving other mission agencies. But soon there were six, then eleven, then eighteen organizations, as well as many internal projects on campus, in one or other of the two buildings the college made available to us.

Then there was the problem of legal papers, and rules for membership, and a governing board, and physical setup. Who would handle the books? Each organization separately, or one general accounting office? How would the rent be divided?

There was a myriad of things to be done, and no one to do them — no one except Ralph, Prudence and myself.

We desperately needed Prudence's help, but where would we find money to pay her? Our salary had now stopped. How were we to live? One of our professor friends was a member of a church mission committee and he took our case to them. That church picked up our support for November and December. Another long time friend, heavily involved in another mission group, promised us a sizeable amount each month to help us with office expenses. October was not the best month to begin raising support since most of the churches with which we were associated had already allocated their mission money by the middle of the month. We sent some urgent letters asking "Help!" and received back some replies of, "Of course," and some "Sorry, too late." Some didn't answer at all. But the Lord provided anyhow.

In a matter of days we had our incorporation papers from the State of California. We were moved in, somewhat comfortably, and began to work.

But it would be some time before the Lord sent the staff we so desperately needed.

9

DECEMBER 1976
GENE DAVIS

It was 17 degrees below zero, and the bitter wind whipped our coats open as we slipped on the icy sidewalks crisscrossing the university campus at Urbana, Illinois. We had come for the triennial Inter-Varsity Missionary Conference where Ralph was a workshop leader and I was to lead a discussion group. The Conference was jammed — 17,000 young people were in attendance and 4,000 had been turned away for lack of space. All classrooms seemed to be wall-to-wall with students, and most workshop leaders were lucky to find the standing room to teach.

It seemed that every hour on the hour everyone was on the move — their destinations all too often quite a distance across the snowy campus. We were no exception. Racing to one class that he was to teach in the Armory, Ralph tried one staircase to find it so jammed he could not get through. He tried another with no more success, and finally was guided by a knowing student up a back staircase, across the hallway, down another stair and up another to reach his class, accessible only by that route. His room was packed, as was the hall and stairs outside his room. He was able to pass only when the students learned that, yes, he was the workshop leader scheduled to speak in that class on the Simple Lifestyle.

One in the hall outside was no ordinary student. He was a veterinary doctor from Portland, Oregon, at the conference because he was the chairman of the missions committee of his church. We found out later that the class topic was of great interest to him because for years he and his family had voluntarily adopted such a lifestyle, giving away a large share of their income to the Lord's work.

Dr. Gene Davis was a determined man. From the moment that class ended Ralph couldn't shake him. He waited for him until all the private questions had been asked and answered. He followed him down the stairs and across the hall where they met me. In order to talk further he insisted on walking with us in the icy cold five blocks across campus to our next meeting, and we slid and shouted above the wind through our mufflers all the way.

"Dave Adams* said for me to get in touch with you. Can you come to our church in

Portland to speak on missions?" Gene shouted.

"Dave Adams, huh? Well, I don't often speak in churches these days. Right now I am very busy, and I don't think Dave Adams realizes just how busy. But on the other hand, I would really like to come. What church is it? When do you want me? For how long?"

That was the beginning of a special, precious friendship. It was also an introduction to a very special church, the Bethlehem Church of Portland. But that story comes later.

---

*Dave is a businessman in Salem, Oregon who came to the School of World Mission for one quarter, got involved with a number of missions projects in the area, and has made repeated trips back to advise and encourage us.

10

JANUARY 1977
"I SIGNED AND SEALED THE DEED"
(Jeremiah 32:10)

"How much money do you need?"

Ralph sucked in his breath and replied, "Ten thousand dollars." Ten thousand at that point was like a million to us. We didn't have it, nor anything even approaching it. We were struggling to pay salaries, the rent, the lights and the phone bill.

Mr. Ottomoeller took out his checkbook, and we watched in amazement at God's grace and timing as he wrote out the check. Morris Watkins, a member of our governing board and director of All Nations Literacy Movement, one of our member organizations, had brought him by Ralph's office that Saturday morning, thinking that he just might find Ralph there.

Now suddenly we had enough to ask for our option!

Just after the turn of the century this Pasadena property had been acquired by a group of godly ministers and laymen who wanted to establish a college to train young men and women for the Lord's service, especially as ministers and missionaries. In 1946 the largest building on campus, the auditorium, had been built. It was the scene of yearly "campmeetings" or spiritual retreats and celebrations. All across the front of this building stretched an old fashioned "mourner's bench" at which people would kneel, in tears confessing their sins and asking God's forgiveness and the infilling of the Holy Spirit. That building, so sacred to many, was still the scene for spiritual exercises — but now in the name of Buddha, the "ascended masters," the "great white brotherhood," Lanello, Krishna, etc. Where strains of "Amazing Grace" once floated, now came chants of "I AM ..." The neighborhood, composed to a large extent of Christians formerly associated with the college, was distressed and incensed.

"How could the college rent to them, much less think of selling to them?" they asked, a note of betrayal in their voices. Their protests were loud and long, and were sent to all levels of the denomination. When we appeared in August of 1976 stating that we would like to buy that campus for a mission center, pastors and parishoners alike breathed a sigh of relief.

Just a few days after we had first spoken to the

college authorities, the cult had submitted the legal papers requesting a two-year lease with an option to buy the campus. It was a great temptation. For three years one negotiation after another had broken down. The college board of trustees needed badly to sell the campus. They doubted that we, so very few and with no great, well-known organization behind us, could raise the money. Yet they knew that the wrath of the Christians in the area would fall on their heads if they sold to the cult. But they had to be responsible trustees of their assets. After extensive deliberations they finally compromised by signing merely the lease presented by the cult but without the statement which said, "with an option to buy."

Ralph knew that the cult would reassert its desire for that option, and at best it would be nip and tuck for us to get it instead. "We have absolutely no future here unless we have an option," he reflected. "But how can we persuade the college to give it to us when we have no money? All we can do is make promises and pray."

One man offered us $5,000 to apply on our option and suggested that we add $10,000 and make an offer to the college. We knew that on an $8.5 million piece of property the usual option payment would be at least $150,000.

But we didn't even have $15,000. Not yet, anyway!

That was when Mr. Ottomoeller walked into our office. He is in the construction business, a

Lutheran who dearly loves the Lord. Once a construction missionary himself, he still visits his brother, a missionary in Africa, to help him with various missionary tasks. And he is a faithful supporter of All Nations Literacy Movement.

Now he was giving us a gift larger than he had ever given to Morris Watkins, the director of All Nations Literacy, and Morris was sitting right there, urging him on, though his organization itself was in great need.

"Are they crazy?" the college authorities must have thought when they saw our check. "Do they think they can get an option for $15,000? Ridiculous!"

And the see-saw began. The college Executive Council voted to give us the option on the basis of the $15,000. So the cult offered $75,000, we were told. Then the entire college board met in special session. We sent a letter reminding the board members that the whole evangelical world (of some 40 million people) was our potential constituency. (The cult, according to hearsay, at best could claim only about 30,000 followers.) The college board confirmed the Council decision, asking us to prepare an option agreement.

Some days later the college lawyer met with ours and went over the agreement line by line. All seemed to be in order. We had it prepared on legal paper and submitted it, and then waited. One week went by, then two, and the signed agreement didn't come. We were very puzzled.

Then we learned that the cult had offered a very large sum as a down payment, to be paid immediately.

How we prayed! We didn't have money like that. Even if they should respond right away, it would take us some time to inform those 40 million evangelicals about our cause. Most of them had never even heard of us. We had no mailing lists. Professional fund raisers had told us it was impossible to raise that much money in six months. Now we needed it in days!

"Oh, Lord. Don't you see our dilemma? You know we can't do this alone. And this large sum is just the beginning. Who are we to even try? But you have called us. You wouldn't give us peace until we came to this place. Won't you help us now?"

Several staff members and concerned college students fasted all that weekend. We didn't know what would result. We knew the odds were strongly against us. But yet we believed God.

On Monday our financial adviser came beaming to our noon prayer time. "Listen to what the Lord said to me over the weekend," he said. "I was praying earnestly on Saturday, much burdened about our situation and not knowing what we should do. All of a sudden a scripture reference came to my mind. I had no idea what on earth that reference could say. It was not a verse I had ever memorized. I just knew that the Lord said to me, 'Look up Jeremiah 32:10' and I did. And this is what it says:

I signed and sealed the deed of purchase before witnesses and weighed out the silver and paid him.

and further on in verses 16 and 17:

Then after I had given the papers to Barach I prayed: "O Lord God! You have made the heavens and earth by your great power; nothing is too hard for you!"

"God will give us this campus. I know He will! Let's just trust Him and wait."

So we waited and prayed and trusted, and worked. We checked some potential sources of large sums of money. We waited through February, and all through March. Finally toward the end of March we were told that, yes, we would get the option.

It was April 15th when the signed document finally arrived in our hands, and to us it was truly a gift from God. We had struggled so many, many months for those simple sheets of paper. Why had it been so hard? We remembered in the Bible where Daniel had fasted and prayed for three weeks, and the angel had come to him, saying "God heard you when you first began to pray, but the Prince of the power of the air hindered." We too had many adversaries, but God had brought us through. How we praised Him!

Now we had only six months to raise at least the first part of a $1.5 million down payment. At last people couldn't laugh at the unreality of our

dream; at least we had the legal option to buy.
But how could we alone, with almost no staff
whatever, be able to even begin to do it?

And God said, "You worry at being so small
and few, but Abraham was only *one* when I
called him." (Isa. 51:2 LB). "With God, everything is possible" (Matt. 19:26b LB).

11

MARCH 1977
STAN PETROWSKI

Months had passed since we moved to the campus. We had been working diligently, building the center organizational structure, seeking tax exemption, trying to obtain the option to buy, interesting mission executives in being consultants and getting on with our job. From time to time we had noticed strange oppressive feelings. It was easy to sympathize with Elijah when he cried out to God, "I, even I only remain" (I Kings 18:22). We often felt totally alone in this battle.

"But it is not a battle of our own choosing," we told ourselves. "Why then do we feel so discouraged?"

It was bad enough when I felt depressed, but when I sensed that many on our staff were unusually discouraged at the same time, I began to examine the situation.

"Is the outlook now more dark than it has been?" My answer was no.

"Is there suddenly more criticism or opposition from some source?" Again the answer was, "Not that I know of."

"Are we all fighting off the flu, perhaps?" And again everyone insisted they were well.

"What is it then?" I asked Prudence. "Why do so many of us feel so down all of a sudden?"

And a light of understanding sprang to her eyes! "So that's what it is!" she said.

"What?" I insisted.

"Several years ago, when I was supervising Campus Crusade's women staff in the Midwest, on several occasions I had experiences of this sort. The first time it happened I was confused, as you are, and then someone pointed out to me that it might be Satanic oppression, and urged me to follow the Biblical pattern of dealing with it. He said we have to remind Satan out loud that in dying on the cross Jesus has already won the victory, that we belong to Him and share in that victory. We must tell Satan that he has no authority at all over us, bind him, and then praise the Lord for our deliverance."

She called the staff together and explained what she felt was happening to us. After prayer we followed the pattern she outlined. It was as if a tremendous burden was lifted from our shoulders. Again we were full of joy and confidence in the Lord. And we thanked God for that lesson.

But we didn't associate this oppression with

Summit until one of the Christians in the community, hired by the college to do work around the campus, informed us that some of our names were tacked onto the base of the large Buddha with a notice that incantations be chanted hourly against us. That was spooky, but too unreal to believe. However, when Stan walked into our office one day in April, we changed our minds.

Two days before, Erik Stadell had brought a letter to Ralph in which someone told of his conversion from this particular cult. We were fascinated by the letter since all we knew to date came from long articles in the local newspaper and bits and pieces picked up from Christian neighbors and friends.

Ralph and I were working on a chapter for a book soon to be published when Erik walked into the office, followed by a pleasant-looking, bearded young man in a light tan sports suit. His bright blue eyes were sparkling as he gripped Ralph's hand and said quietly, "I'm just praising the Lord. I'm so glad you're the ones here."

Stan Petrowski told us he had felt led of the Lord to come to Pasadena to see what the Church Universal and Triumphant (Summit) was doing. "I walked through the campus and then decided to see what the neighbors felt about this group. So I knocked on a door down the street. The people there happened to be Lutherans and they told me that you people in this one building on this side of the street are Christians, and that I should come to see you. So here I am."

And this is the story he told us.

About eight years earlier Stan had been born again through contact with a few Christians who helped him when his life was in a shambles. Almost immediately afterward he had moved from the West Coast to Pennsylvania, where he knew no one and where he set up a health food store as a way to support himself and also to attain the physical purity he sought. There he tried to grow in his newly found faith, alone and without Christian guidance of any kind. And there he was led astray.

People of all sorts came into his store looking for health food. Some came in to distribute "health literature." Among this literature was the *Aquarian New Testament,* which he was urged to read, and the Chinese book of divination called *I Ching.* Being a new Christian, all alone, Stan was not wise enough to recognize the additions to and misinterpretations of scripture included in the *Aquarian New Testament,* nor did anyone warn him of the dangers of becoming involved with *I Ching* and yoga. Over a period of time which involved contact with various psychic and religious organizations, he finally found himself in the Summit International headquarters (which he called "a monastery"), located at that period in Colorado Springs, Colorado. There the mixture of meditation, yoga, mantras, scripture and psychic practices coincided perfectly with his recent experiences. And unlike others he had known who were involved in such phenomena, these people were highly ethical, well-dressed, and stressed physical purity through abstinence from meat, alcohol, tobacco and drugs. He was troubled only by their emphasis on wealth and their obvious materialism.

Summit told him that the Bible was inaccurate, that ancient copyists had left out many things that were in the original documents of the early centuries. These left-out portions were dictated to the leader of their movement (Mark Prophet) by people now "ascended."

Stan rose in the Summit International movement until he was one of their top staff. At that point he had the ability to read other people's minds and, to a certain extent, could even control their thought processes. This was all done through spirit power — an unholy spirit power — he told us much later. Eventually he was sent to India and Nepal to visit a number of monasteries in order to incorporate into the cult's teaching the "truths" from Buddhism and Hinduism. But all this time he was hungry for the true and living God.

After four years, Stan left the organization and then on his own returned to Nepal, searching for his own "personal guru" who, he said, had contacted him psychically. He walked barefoot in the snow for 200 miles, visiting monastery after monastery, only to realize that what (or who) he sought was not there. One day, trekking across a high mountain pass in the Himalayas, stumbling in the snow toward yet another Buddhist monastery, he fell on his knees and cried out, "Oh, God, what is true?" Prostrate in the snow, in tears, he felt a Presence he had not known before, and heard Someone say to him, "I, Jesus, am the way. I am the truth. I am the life. No man comes to the Father but by me." He was stunned! At the Summit monastery he had often chanted the first part of that phrase, but the last part had not been there. There the "I AM" had referred to some god-presence which he himself was becoming. Now Jesus was saying that Only He was the way, the truth and the life. Moreover, *there was no other way to the Father but by Him.* He remembered that experience long years ago in Portland. That, then, had been the true way, and he had wandered so far, so needlessly.

Three days later he arrived at the monastery, but knew in his heart that the One who had spoken to him on the way was the One he had so long sought. After waiting out a small snow storm, he left abruptly and returned to the States. There, after days of prayer and fasting, he was led to a group of Christians who laid hands on him and prayed. For the first time in years he felt released from the spirit of oppression which only later did he realize had been demonic. In his own words, "I went through a process of systematically renouncing every false religion that I had ever been involved in, in the name of Jesus Christ." It took long months of Bible study and many, many hours of communion with God before he learned to distinguish between the spirits. But now he is a burning witness to God's power to rescue His own from the clutches of the "false prophets." He spends his time on the road, warning Christians and witnessing to young people caught up in the cults.

We sat there in our office, fascinated and yet appalled, listening to Stan. The world he told us of was one we didn't know and couldn't understand.

"When I knew that Summit was here, and that you Christians were across the street from them, I wondered just how much you knew about the group."

"Essentially nothing at all," Ralph replied. We've been told it's an American group which practices Hindu philosophy. But aside from a few newspaper articles, that's all we know."

"Yes, I'm not surprised," Stan volunteered. "Here, let me tell you a bit."

He took more than an hour, talking about chants that have an unholy spiritual power, of "balancing karma", of communication with people now dead and with powers in the spirit world, of incantations, mantras . . .

We were quiet, too shocked to know what to say, and a bit unbelieving perhaps. All we had wanted to do was to buy this campus and to set in motion a new wave of mission interest that would complete the task of world evangelization. Had we also stumbled into a confrontation with the occult?

"What can we do?" I blurted out.

"You just claim Christ's victory. And you

pray. This situation is going to take a lot of prayer power." And he touched his knees as he looked straight into our eyes.

"You'll pray for us, too, won't you?" we suggested.

"I'll pray for you every day. I know what you're going through. I could tell when I walked in that the devil's been giving you a rough time. But God's on the throne. Don't forget that. And Christ has already won the victory."

We prayed briefly together and then Stan was gone, to reappear again, unannounced, at the very end of June, the day before the cult's largest conference of the year was to begin.

12

APRIL 15, 1977
"ARE YE ABLE? . . ."
(Matthew 20:22)

The day we finally got our option to buy the campus, Ralph and I left for Portland. This trip was the result of the icy walk across the campus that December day in Illinois.

Gene Davis's church met in what was formerly an Elk's lodge near Lake Oswego in Portland. There was nothing "churchy" about the building in the traditional sense. It was set in the middle of rolling hills and pastures, a sprawled-out building built of natural wood. Inside where the main hall had become the sanctuary, the people sat in a huge semi-circle around a low platform.

Even the service was nontraditional. Instead of hymns, the congregation sang choruses and "songs of the Spirit." There was no organ. The atmosphere was relaxed and warm. "It is a Baptist church," Ralph had told me earlier. "Most of its members are new converts with very little church background of any sort."

We had arrived in Portland on Thursday evening, and our hosts had driven us by the church on our way from the airport. All weekend, we were told, was scheduled. Friday morning Ralph was to speak at a prayer breakfast for the church staff. Friday evening he would attend a men's dinner where again he would say a few words. Meanwhile I would be speaking to a group of women at the church. Saturday morning Ralph would be at a men's breakfast and in the afternoon I would attend a mother-daughter tea at the church. Saturday night we were invited to dinner at a local restaurant with several couples from the church. Sunday Ralph would speak to a Sunday School class, and then at the two morning services, say a few words at the luncheon after the services, and speak again that evening.

It was an exhausting but a great weekend. Friday morning was free for me, and I had a great time of spiritual refreshment. At one o'clock I was taken to Gene Davis' home. His wife, Vivian, was still washing dishes when I walked in, and I immediately felt at home. Gene and Vivian are "parents" to about eight or ten young adults not related to them as well as to their own children. Each of these youths had come to them as to a refuge, seeking relief from some great spiritual or emotional stress and yearning for a stable home. Vivian and Gene had accepted this ministry as God's calling. From time to time over the years we had had someone not related to us living with us for awhile, and I marveled at Vivian's calmness and her unselfish willingness to share her home with so many live-ins. Both she and Gene were gifted with an ususual firmness mixed with great kindness when dealing with the personal emotional stresses and personality deficiencies of their "family." 'Vivian obviously is a person of great strength and a cheerful disposition," I thought. But later I learned that at one time, long before she had accepted this calling, she had felt terribly depressed, a total failure. God had touched her and prepared her for this unique ministry so that she now asserted that she didn't see how she could make it without all those other members of her household. What a great couple!

All afternoon Vivian and I fellowshipped together, praising the Lord for what he had taught each of us — lessons sometimes very alike, sometimes very different, but always just right for each of us. As the afternoon wore on I found it hard to concentrate on the conversation. I needed to steal away somewhere to get my talk into shape. I had done almost no public speaking for over two years — indeed couldn't speak at all for six months of that time, and I felt totally inadequate now to stand in front of a group. I felt ill-prepared in every way. God would have to help me.

That evening I felt that God met with us. We were not many, but those women were women who knew how to pray. They must have been praying for me for suddenly all my nervous tension left me, as I started to talk.

I had been impressed late that afternoon with the fact that God is pleased when we dare to trust him for the difficult, seemingly ridiculous things that He wants to do. Even as parents love to do hard things for their children, God loves to prove Himself for us. It had been His design that Moses should lead those newly released Hebrew slaves through a wilderness where there was neither water nor food or any sort. God wanted them to learn that He is all sufficient. It had been by His command that Gideon sent home a huge army, retaining a band of only 300 to fight against a great army. God had wanted them to learn that He doesn't have to depend on huge numbers of well-trained men to win victories. God had allowed a giant to confront the Israelites so that a young boy, bringing a lunch to his soldier brothers, could remind God's people that one smooth stone whirled in His name and under His guidance can put an entire army to flight.

The Bible is full of such examples — Jeremiah, "only a youth" as he himself insisted, yet willing to stand against the crowd and declare God's judgment unless they repented; Stephen, preaching his sermon while the stones fell against his body; Paul . . . All had great faith because over and over again they were willing to risk all they had, knowing that God would be utterly faithful to them in their need.

I don't know what those women learned that night I spoke in Portland, but God was talking to me as He talked through me. Those thoughts were not my thoughts. And as I talked I again pondered our own situation. Was I willing to risk our all — our financial security, our home, our reputation, our friends, our future, even my husband's life, perhaps, if the strain should prove to be too great? Could God become everything to me without need for anything beyond what He chose to give me from His own hand? Could I trust Him that much?

A great peace flooded over me as I remembered His great faithfulness in the past: a few weeks earlier, I had had surgery for a tumor on my arm. The scar was still angry and itched, but there was no cancer. The severed nerve which had caused my loss of voice the year before He had overruled and I could speak. The year before that our family sat rejoicing in our wrecked car, so very grateful that God had spun us into a tree on the right rather than allow us to go over into a deep canyon on the left of the highway. That night I thanked the Lord for our beautiful and godly four daughters. When so many teenagers were rebellious, God had given us these darling girls — the greatest gift of all: Beth, Becky, Linda and Tricia.

13

APRIL 17, 1977
SMALL CHURCH—
BIG CHALLENGE

I gasped to myself when Ralph said it. "Surely he's speaking tongue-in-cheek. He can't expect a church this size, this far away from Pasadena to give us $100,000, and in less than six months. These people have just met us. How can they put that kind of trust in us — even if they have that kind of money? And how can they have that kind of money? Surely Ralph can't really mean that!"

But he was continuing. "If a church like yours with only 200 giving units gives that sacrificially, it will put all those two and three-thousand-member churches to shame. Your gift will be much more than the money. It will be a challenge to every other church that hears about the project."

"He really means it!" I thought.

"Now why should you here in Portland be interested in a project in Pasadena?" he went on. "Why should you be interested in those 2.4 billion people of whom I've been speaking? Why should it matter to you if they ever hear the gospel as you have?"

"It matters to you because it matters to God, and you cannot be God's children without being concerned about His concerns. To put it more simply, God loves those mountaineers in Turkey, the Kurds. For decades now they have been slaughtered by the Turks, and now are not even able to find the refuge they once had in Iran. They are Muslims, but their enemies are also Muslims, and perhaps, for the first time in history the Kurds are willing to hear about another way. Jesus loves them just as much as He loves you and me. He wants them to know Him. He wants to bring them peace. There are thousands of groups of people around the world equally dear to God, whom no one is reaching — not the mission societies, not the national churches. We have a gospel, given to us at great cost, which has turned our lives around, given us hope and joy. It can also bring them new life. Do you remember what Jesus' last command to His disciples was before He ascended into heaven? It was to go into all the world and to make disciples of all the peoples (all the ethnic units) of the earth. That is why you can't just shrug this off and say, 'It's no concern of mine. I have enough to do here at home.' If it is your Father's concern, it has also to be yours."

"That's pretty heavy," I thought, seated halfway back in the congregation. "Can people in a Sunday morning church service take it that straight? But then Jesus had laid it on pretty heavy too. 'Unless you are willing to leave father and mother . . . you cannot be my disciple.' Ralph was not asking them to 'leave', he was just asking them to take up their responsibilities as children of God to 'care'."

The service was soon over, and as usual the people gathered around Ralph to ask questions. Again, as usual, many of them were young people, challenged, ready to begin to count the cost personally. "Will the more mature members shrug it off as they do in so many churches?" I asked myself. "Dear God, we have done our best. Now you continue to speak to them," I prayed.

14

MAY 1977
"MY GOD WILL SUPPLY
ALL YOUR NEEDS"
(Philippians 4:19)

It hit us all like a ton of bricks. We had been working and praying so hard, trying to get the legal option to buy, that we had thought little about what next. But now it hit us. "We have exactly five months to raise $850,000, the first part of the $1.5 million needed for a down payment. What do we do?"

There were still such a pitifully few of us on staff, and most were part-time volunteers. We knew we couldn't start raising money without getting public backing from well-known people — and that would involve Ralph in endless phone calls, hundreds of letters, and much, much prayer. How could we possibly do it?

It took all of May and into June to line up consultants, people whom others trusted who would vouch for us when asked about our project. Every Sunday at church friends would question, "How is it going? How much money have you raised?" At first I appreciated their concern, but as the weeks went by and we were spending most of our time lining up consultants, I wanted to avoid them. The time was getting short. How we knew that! But we also knew that without the interested concern of well-known mission experts, we could go nowhere.

I don't know what we would have done without Ralph's secretary, Prudence. She had come to Ralph's office at the seminary the year before, admitting somewhat apologetically that she wasn't a great typist. But she had been told that Ralph was looking for someone to organize. him. She thought she could do that. She was truly God's gift to us. She was office manager, public relations director, personnel manager, social hostess, chaplain — all at the same time. If we needed something, she "just happened" to know someone or something about it. Best of all, she was a person of faith, unafraid to tackle hard things.

But she was also human. Just how much can one person carry? I was working every day alongside Ralph and Prudence, but the job was just too great, even with those wonderful volunteers who had come for a few weeks or months.

One Saturday in early June Ralph was working alone in his office while I tackled the accumulated undone tasks at home. The office phone rang and one of his newly named consultants, a well-known mission executive, called him with a host of suggestions, all good. About half-way down the list, Ralph stopped him, cold.

"Those are great ideas, but how can we implement them?"

"What do you mean?" the caller asked. "Haven't I just told you how?"

"One thing you forgot. I have no staff. I've just finished typing a letter to our consultants. While I'm talking to you, I'm stuffing envelopes and licking stamps. And then I'll drive this mailing to the Post Office. I agree that I should do all you suggest, but I just can't!"

There was a shocked silence on the other end of the line, then, "Listen, brother, I'll put in the mail right now a check for $3,000. That will pay for a secretary for you for awhile. And when that is gone, I'll send some more. Now can you find a good secretary?"

That was how Jane came to us. As June progressed our winter part-time volunteers left for summer jobs or summer studies, and the Lord filled their places, usually with seminarians or college students, often from far away. Most of them we had never heard of, and we wondered how they knew of us. Gwen came from Minneapolis after learning of us through a mutual friend. Our daughter in Boston and her husband in seminary at Gordon-Conwell saw

"Star Wars" one night and said, "What are we doing here when there's a great battle in progress in Pasadena?" And they brought with them Hal and Liz and Dave and Debbie.

Ralph spoke at a conference in the Midwest and a young businessman dropped all for "two weeks" (but stayed for three months)! He spoke at a church in San Diego, and Jeff, on a visit to his grandmother, responded to the challenge. Most of these people were short-term helpers: we called them our "90-day wonders." And they were wonders. They helped in all sorts of spots and all sorts of ways. Young people who had never written anything more important than a term paper were busily at work on publicity brochures, newspaper releases, pamphlets and seminar programs.

It was a time of stretching for all of us. At times Prudence, Ralph and I felt like Moses with his motley crew. We had people gathered from all over, from all sorts of churches, working at tasks they had never attempted under the direction of people who had never managed others. Could God bring anything out of that mess?

You'd better believe it!

15

MAY 20, 1977
"AND THE LORD ADDED
TO THE 'CHURCH' DAILY"
(Acts 2:47)

Almost every day now there were changes.
Our list of people who had agreed to be consultants grew from week to week. By May 13th
we had 16: the list included seminary professors, executives of mission boards, directors
of associations of mission societies, etc.* Already
it was a "who's who" among mission strategists.
Very early, some of these, unsolicited, wrote
warm letters of encouragement. One such was
from Donald Hoke, director of the newly established Billy Graham Center for Evangelism,
who wrote that the USCWM is "probably the
single most strategic institution and movement
in the world today, aimed at evangelizing the
two billion persons who can only be reached by
cross-cultural, 'missionary' evangelism."

We had to reprint new stationery almost every week to keep up with the changes. Not only was the list of consultants at the bottom of the page constantly (and rapidly) growing, the list of staff personnel down the side was also getting longer. On May 27th Hal Leaman's name appeared on the list as the new Associate General Director.

Hal was a hard-headed businessman, not easily persuaded. He had born in him a New England reticence about West Coast wild ideas, bolstered by a number of years in an even more conservative Europe. Some years earlier the Lord had called him to begin a new type of Christian ministry in Europe, and he had just graduated from Gordon-Conwell seminary as the completion of the first phase toward that goal.

"Can you take out a few months to help us?" Ralph pled. "Two years from now we can probably get along without you, but we are really desperate for help now."

It took some persuasion. Hal had long lists of questions that first needed answering. But by the end of May he had agreed to come, and was added to our letterhead before even arriving.

Further down the side of the stationery a new department of mission training was added to the services the Center would perform. This was the Nurse Practioner's Program to be headed by Liz, Hal's wife.

Every week now Ralph sent a VIP letter to consultants or possible consultants and under the date always indicated how many weeks we had left before our down-payment was due. The consultants also asked hard questions, which Ralph circulated to all the others along with his answers:

"Why do you feel you need a college campus?"

(In short) "We expect to have hundreds of students from secular schools coming for one semester."

"Why this particular campus in Pasadena?"

(In short) "There is a larger concentration of nationalities in this area than anywhere else in the world . . . with implications for training and other strategies. Also, this campus is available. To build it would cost more than twice as much."

And so on.

By now Prudence, in consultation with the Board of Directors of the Center (and especially with Ralph) had worked out the membership application form for organizations wanting to become a part of the Center. To be eligible, the applying organization had to have the same goals as ours — evangelizing the beyond-reach "hidden peoples" of the earth — and had to agree with our theological, management and lifestyle standards. Some who easily qualified could not come — they needed more space than we had available. Our standards were high, yet every few weeks we had more and more applications and soon 16 different incorporated or unincorporated organizations became members.

Even our name was changed from the World

Mission Center to the U.S. Center for World Mission when one of our consultants pointed out (and we agreed) that the newer name would avoid the impression that we meant to manage the earth. We had long expected other nations to need and want to establish similar centers focusing exclusively on frontier populations. Already Ralph was scheduled to take part in a conference of bishops of the Church of South India scheduled for August, and on that trip he hoped to be able to persuade someone to do for India what we were trying to do for the United States. (It worked. A fledgling board was agreed upon for a "South India Center for World Mission.")

We were greatly encouraged by the increasing interest and staff. We still were as poor as ever, but buoyed up by faith. Our dream was so huge — but the need was even larger. That was plain to us. Could we help others to see that?

Some did. Paul Orjala, the Professor of Missions at the Nazarene Theological Seminary wrote: "Not since the demise of the Kennedy School of Missions at Hartford Seminary has anything loomed on the missions horizon of such magnitude and potential. To be frank, it is almost frightening in its scope, but I guess that is part of the specifications of anything momentous that God challenges us to undertake with His guidance and strength. I have found myself compelled to prayer for you and for the others involved."

How we depended on those prayers!

*Some of the early ones to agree to be consultants were Jack Frizen, Executive Director of the Interdenominational Foreign Mission Association, Harold Lindsell, Editor of Christianity Today, David Howard, the organizer of the famous Urbana Student Missionary Conferences, Donald McGavran founder and Dean Emeritus of the School of World Mission at Fuller Seminary, George Peters, Professor of Missions at Dallas Seminary, Waldron Scott, Executive Director of the World Evangelical Fellowship, J. Christy Wilson, Professor of Missions at Gordon Conwell Seminary and formerly pastor of the only Christian church in Afganistan, and Donald Hoke, Director of the newly established Billy Graham Center for Evangelism.

16

JUNE 15, 1977
BETHLEHEM'S STAR

The phone rang early that Saturday morning. Gene Davis, on the other end, was very excited.

"Ralph, when you were up here last April you said something about getting several churches to put up $100,000 apiece toward the purchase of the campus? Well, I'm coming down with our pastor and three of our key laymen to talk it over with you!"

"Man, that's great," Ralph said.

"Well, don't count on anything yet. This is just an exploratory trip, but the Lord is working. Fred, our pastor, has to preach in Chula Vista on Sunday the 24th, and he has suggested we come there on Thursday or Friday to see the campus and talk about it. How about that?"

"That's wonderful, really wonderful! Let me look at my calendar to see if I'll be here. Hmmm . . . I have one or two little things, but they are local and can be easily changed. So come on down. We'll be ready for you."

The five men arrived on schedule. Gene, I knew from our visit up there. John Patterson, the young realtor, I remembered from our ten-minute stop at his housewarming. Pastor Fred was the tall, sandy-haired man with the beautiful singing voice and the warm, loving spirit. I could not have forgotten him. The other two were new to me, but I came to respect why they also had been chosen for this trip.

It was an all-day affair, lasting into the evening and the next morning. Before disbanding Fred said, "Brothers, we must pray about this. What Ralph is asking us to do is far more than we can humanly do. But we have a big God. It is not too big for Him. Let us pray now, and then go on our way, and trust the Lord to show us what He wants us to do."

As he had in his home in Portland, Gene knelt with his head touching the floor. It was a precious time with each other and with the Lord. And we pledged together to pray aloud for fifteen minutes every day that the Lord would give us this campus.

It was several days after the five returned to Portland before we heard again from Gene. "We talked about that $100,000 all the way home and have prayed much about it. We've decided the Lord wants us to raise it, even if we have to mortgage our church property. The Lord will make this a blessing to us, we feel sure."

Our staff was walking on air when we heard the news. It was almost July, and we still had, all together, only about $25,000. We had been praying that the Lord would give us the entire down payment of $1.5 million and were reluctant to pay the required $850,000 on October 1st unless we could "see" the balance just around the corner.

The sky above us was dark with only one bit of light — that first large pledge from the Bethlehem Church. "How well-named that church is," I said to Ralph. "Though small, 'least among' the churches, one might say, still it is like a star to lead the way to a faith where one cannot see."

17

JUNE 1977
THE CHURCH UNIVERSAL
AND TRIUMPHANT

June — already! Uppermost in our hearts and minds was the fact that in a few weeks our down payment was due. Now that we had a list of at least thirty well-known and respected Christian leaders who were willing to act as our consultants, we could appeal to the evangelical public for financial backing. Now at last we had the staff to be able to start sending letters, writing news releases, contacting churches, setting up promotional luncheons, and processing gifts. Even with the extremely welcome additional help we were BUSY!

Since Stan's visit in March we had been less overcome by depression. Now we recognized our foe and were able instantly to rebuke him in the name of Jesus, whose blood we claimed for our protection and for our sufficiency. And we kept on working, happily.

Some of our new staff from time to time

bought various pieces of Summit literature, and many of us studied them, trying to see what was taught across the street from us. We found these a confusing mixture of Hindu philosophy and terminology mixed up with quotations and names from the Bible. Jesus was often mentioned, but in many ways extremely foreign to historical and Biblical Christianity. The booklets spoke of Mrs. Prophet as "the Divine Mother" and "the Mother of the Flame," reminding us of the ever-present bumper stickers: "Souls of great light are waiting to be born. Have one. (signed) Mother" and "Abortion is first degree murder of God." The literature spoke of communications from St. Germain, whose picture was always prominently displayed and who seemed to be the guiding light. Mrs. Prophet spoke of receiving messages from the Archangel Michael, Buddha, Jesus, and other "ascended masters" including her dead husband, Mark Prophet, otherwise known as Lanello. Decisions were sometimes submitted to "the Darjeeling Council" and letters were written to "chelas" around the world. The more we read the more we could understand how inquirers could be confused. Bible references were common but often incorrectly quoted and always grossly misinterpreted. We wondered how Americans, who have so much chance to come to know the truth, get involved in such philsophical nonsense.

Then some of our staff accepted the invitation to attend the Friday night "open meeting" to which the neighborhood had been invited.

18

9 P.M., JULY 1, 1977
"YOU FIGHT . . . AGAINST SPIRITUAL DARKNESS"
(Ephesians 6:12)

Holy Cosmos' violet ray (3x)
Work thy power through me, I pray (3x)

Holy Cosmos' yellow ray (3x)
Touch and heal, and light my way (3x)

Holy Cosmos' celestial ray (3x)
Fill me with thy love today (3x)*

The chanting grew almost deafening. Brad found himself automatically tapping his foot to the rhythm. Jud and Walter sat together, as did Hal and Liz, Beth and Brad, Bruce and Christy, Stan and Sandee. They had gone to the meeting two by two, sitting widely apart, and they prayed that Christ would protect them from any power the spirits would try to exercise over them.

We were all very curious. What would their public meeting be like? Would it be so "Eastern" that the average American would have culture shock, or would it be rather similar to the average Protestant church service?

Ralph was out of town, returning the next morning. I felt definitely that God did not want me to go to that public meeting of Summit. I don't know whether I felt this way because as Ralph's wife there might be more Satanic attack on me, or why. I just knew I was *not* to go. Becky also knew she shouldn't go. For a long time she had not been really well. She had graduated, exhausted, two weeks earlier from college, and felt unprepared physically for a battle with spiritual forces. Bob had gone home to change into a suit, and had missed the pairing off two by two which Prudence had advised for those who would attend. Now he appeared, wanting to go, but having no partner.

I was especially concerned about Bob's going by himself. He had grown up a Roman Catholic and a few years earlier had come into a personal experience with Christ while a student at Caltech. Being scientifically trained, he tended at that point not to really believe in "principalities and powers in high places" that would war against our spirits. It was somehow too superstitious, too medieval. "So, there is no one to go with me," he said to me. "After all, what can happen? I'll be O.K." and he went alone.

"As we entered," Christy was to write later, "there were two guys and a girl up front with a guitar, singing 'mantras' — very Eastern-sounding. They would start out slowly, and as the short phrases were repeated again and again, they gained momentum, until the mantra seemed firmly implanted in one's mind and the atmosphere became intoxicating. Everyone seemed to be effectively drawn into a mood of receptivity. There was a feeling of anticipation in the crowd." Later on the choir had sung a song about Jesus, one which could easily have been sung in any evangelical Sunday service.

Then Elizabeth Clare Prophet had risen and begun the chant, instructing newcomers and visitors how to participate. It had begun low at first, and the words were distinct and clear. Over and over again the same phrases had been repeated. But now voices were louder, words more blurred, the chanting more rapid.

Bob, of our staff seated alone, felt its mesmerizing effect and began to pray, quietly at first and then aloud. It flashed through his mind that the devil was using rhythm to work a spell on these people, so that they could more easily be deceived, and he determined to break that rhythm. All around him people were shouting louder and louder:

Ho-ly Cos-mos' vi-olet ray
Work thy pow'r through me, I pray . . .

Bob started to pray louder and louder in non-rhythmic pattern, totally out of beat with the rest of the audience. The lady beside him became quite agitated.

"No," she said as she leaned toward him, "No, that's not the way! Here, here are the words. Say them with us."

Bob ignored her and continued praying.

"Listen," she insisted more loudly, "you won't feel the vibrations if you don't do it right!"

Suddenly the chanting was at an end and the audience was dismissed for a fifteen minute break before "the Mother" would give a dictation from Lanello, her dead husband, now an "ascended master."

Bob almost ran from the building, praising God for what he felt to be a deliverance from Satanic power.

Beth came back across the street and started repeating the chant. "Beth, how can you?" her husband asked in shock. "Why did you memorize it?"

"I didn't mean to. I didn't chant, but those words and that rhythm just stick in your mind. I can see how people get sucked in, thinking it is innocent, when it is really calling to something other than God. Never will I feel that chanting is just a simple religious game."

---

*Because all chants used by the cult are copyrighted, this is not an actual quote, but is similar in sense and meter to several actually used.

19

JULY 3, 1977
A POWER ENCOUNTER

That weekend was both physically draining and spiritually exciting. Several weeks previous the college had informed us that some of those attending the Summit conference would be staying in the dormitory where our offices were located, and by Friday our building was full. We had placed several booklets in our front entry through which they had to pass, and we noticed that the Inter-Varsity one entitled "Buddha, Zoraster or Christ" was the one most often picked up. After office hours on Friday and Monday and most of Saturday and Sunday many of our staff sat on our patio lawn singing and praying, and we noticed that a number of those attending the conference stopped just inside their doorways to listen. Only one ventured to join us, and she invited us to come to hear their "dictation from Jesus" which Elizabeth Clare Prophet was to receive that coming Sunday.

On Friday Stan and his wife Sandee had returned to the campus. Because most of our staff were newly arrived, Ralph asked Stan to explain to us the Summit teachings so that we would know how to respond to questions anyone attending the conference might ask us. Again we were impressed by how far from the Bible those teachings were.

Early Saturday morning Stan took his place on the corner across the street to the west of our building. He didn't want Summit to blame the U.S. Center for World Mission for his witness, and rarely came near our building that entire weekend. In one hand he supported a large sign which read, "Who are the gods?"

"What do you mean by your sign?" asked a blond-haired girl wearing a conference badge, and he started to explain the gospel to her. "I am a Christian. I've been filled with the Spirit," she assured Stan.

"Then what are you doing here?" Stan asked. And he started to explain to her the different teachings of Summit and to compare them with scripture.

Almost immediately twenty to thirty people gathered around them, listening. Some were Summit staff, "guards" we came to call them, because they repeatedly tried to silence Stan or to get those listening to him to leave. From that hour until the end of the conference they maintained a watch over Stan, two following him everywhere he went and two sitting on the lawn across the street on the main campus, palms up, chanting decrees against him, Stan said.

"Elizabeth would never let them talk to me," he told us. "But just think! Because they have to guard me, they hear everything I say to anyone. I get to preach the gospel to them over and over. Isn't that wonderful?" he beamed.

At one point a police car drove up, stopped and checked out the situation but apparently found that Stan was doing nothing illegal.

We had been singing and praying, constantly it seemed. By Sunday some of our younger staff members were becoming restless, anxious to bear a more definite witness. But the moment they crossed the street, Bibles in hand, they were ushered off and threatened with a call to the police.

"I hope other Christians are able to witness to these people," Beth sighed. "It seems we can't get near them. Even those staying on our campus rush past us, in and out of the building, almost as if they've been told not to speak to us."

"But God can do more things through prayer than we have any idea of," I said. "They can't keep us from praying."

Monday was the last day of the conference, and by nightfall Bruce had decided that he wanted to try something else. He sought Stan out and talked to him about his idea.

"Stan, you know one of our organizations rents the upper floor of Science on the main campus. That's just outside the entrance to the auditorium where the conference is being held.

What do you think about some of us going over there to pray? We won't sing or pray out loud. We won't disturb their meeting. We will just go there and pray quietly. What do you say?"

"That's a marvelous idea. You know, it is important to them that they be able to control the air waves — the 'energies' and the forcefield surrounding the auditorium. Only thus can they hear from the 'ascended masters', from Buddha, Jesus, Sanat Kumara, Magda, St. Germain, and so on. There is a host of them. Only thus can Elizabeth Clare Prophet receive her dictations from the spirit world. But if you fill the air with prayers, these dictations cannot reach her, those spirits cannot get through to her with their messages."

So Bruce obtained permission from the organization which rented that building.

At 6 P.M. we met on the lawn in our patio as usual, and prayed and sang, trusting that somehow God would use our efforts to defeat the enemy in his efforts to deceive these people, many of whom we now knew were members of Christian churches. Neither Ralph nor I knew what the young people planned to do. Ralph, just back from a long trip, was busy in his office, and I was very weary after the long work days and the evenings and weekend spent almost entirely in spiritual combat through prayer and singing. We were very aware that a spiritual struggle was in process, even though Stan, who was not of our staff, was the only one we knew overtly involved with Summit people in discussions of any length at all. Throughout those months previous, and even more during those days, we had become acutely aware of what Jesus meant when He said, "Ask anything *in my name*." Many of us had heard that phrase all our lives and always closed our prayers with the words "in Jesus name." But that weekend we became more conscious of the *power* of the *name* of Jesus in combating unseen spiritual forces.

The meeting in the auditorium started early this last night of the conference. Every other evening loud chanting could be heard for blocks, starting about 9 P.M.: "I AM the way; I AM the truth; I AM the life; I AM the resurrection; I AM in me, my very own beloved Christ self," and always ending with a thrice repeated, mesmerizing refrain such as "I AM the Word of God, I AM the Word of God, I AM the Word of God incarnate."

That night there was no chanting; all was strangely silent. As a group of our young people rose from the lawn to go across the street to the Science building, three Summit staff leaders walked briskly up our patio sidewalk, back to Ralph's office which he had left only minutes before. They passed our young people leaving for their campus. I watched the two groups, seemingly oblivious of each other, headed in opposite directions. I wondered what I should do — stop the young people, or talk to the Summit leaders? I didn't know where Ralph was (he had gone to another office to type a letter) and I prayed for guidance. I wanted the young people to follow their own guidance in witnessing and prayer, yet I did not want us to be guilty of trespassing nor of antagonizing Summit. Already we were blamed for any witnessing done by anybody, no matter whether we had ever heard of the person (or group) or not. Almost always we had known of this witness only after it had happened.

But this situation was quite obviously out of my hands and Ralph's.

Our young people told me later, "We had barely reached the steps of Science when the men who had walked into our building came back across the street and saw us there."

"What are you doing here," one of them asked.

"We're praying."

"Praying? What for?"

"We're praying for the meeting in the auditorium."

"What are you praying for that for?"

"We're praying that the people will really come to know Jesus Christ as the only One who can forgive their sins."

One Summit guard, rather disturbed, asked, "Are you willing to submit your prayers to the will of God?"

"Certainly" Bruce answered, not really understanding what the question meant.

By this time six other pastel-clad guards had joined the three, and attempted to engage the young people in theological argument. But Bruce interposed "We didn't come over here to argue. We only want to pray. We will do it silently. We won't bother you."

"No, you must get off this campus or we'll call the police."

"No," Bruce answered. "The offices upstairs belong to one of our organizations, and we have been invited by them to come here to pray."

The guards moved away and conferred together. Then they returned and one shook his finger at them and shouted, "In the name of the eternal Christ-self I order you to cease praying and to leave this campus!"

The young Christians would have been amazed at the oddity of using Christ's name to stop someone from praying had they not been so intent in their own prayers while Bruce talked. Nobody moved. It was a deadlock.

The guards moved away again to confer among themselves, and when they returned Bruce said, "Look, we don't want to make you angry. We'll just go on upstairs and have our prayer meeting there."

And they did. They prayed and sang quietly for an hour or more, binding Satan in his efforts to deceive the people so near them and yet so far from the truth of the Bible. They rejoiced in the sense of the presence of the Lord there with them in that "upper room."

It was nearing 11 P.M. and still there had been no chanting that evening. Suddenly there was a knock on the door. It was locked, as was the door on the ground floor entrance, but when Bruce opened it, three cult leaders entered. "We just thought we would stop by and say hello," the only woman said.

"Is this an opportunity to witness, sent by God, or is it a ploy to distract us from praying so that their medium can receive another 'dictation' from the spirit world?" Bruce wondered, and urged some to continue in prayer.

Valerie, the woman, asked why they were praying. "After all, we're Christians just like you."

"If you are, then you also believe that Jesus is the *only* begotten Son of God, the only One who can take away our sins," Jud, a Christian from the neighborhood, answered. And he opened his Bible to John 3:16. "Do you believe that?"

"We believe that Jesus is God. But the Bible says, "Ye are all gods," one answered, but he couldn't remember the Biblical reference.

This new theological debate, for such it was, lasted for sometime while three continued praying off in one corner. Our people talked about the Garden of Eden, about Satan's attempt to be "like God," about his tempting Eve with the words, "God knows that the instant you eat the fruit, you will become like Him" (Genesis 3:4). They were amazed at how the Holy Spirit brought the right Bible references to their minds at the right time. They truly felt the Holy Spirit was speaking through them.

The Summit people seemed to recognize that the only authority our young people would accept was the Bible and thus tried to quote from it several times. But they obviously didn't know it very well. One said at one point, "Like the Bible says, 'God helps those who help themselves.'"

Nobody even smiled when Bruce pointed out that this phrase wasn't from the Bible, but later when our young people recounted it to us, they all burst into laughter.

It was also clear that the Summit people were trying to find out who was behind the U.S. Center for World Mission. They questioned each of our group, one by one, as to their church connections, and could hardly believe that almost every one came from a different church. They were even more incredulous when they learned that people of many different denominations all over the nation were praying for us and shared completely a single Biblical faith.

The discussion lasted for more than an hour. Almost as if she were watching a clock, Valerie suddenly said, "I think we can leave now."

"Let us pray with you first. May we?" Bob asked.

They seemed ill at ease, momentarily at a loss as to how to respond, but assented. Each Christian prayed a few sentences, asking the Lord to make himself real to these people. They wanted them to meet the real Jesus, not the "angel of light" who called himself by that name and led them astray.

Alex, one of the cult leaders, prayed too, but he obviously felt ill at ease. His prayer was part chant, part prayer — eyes wide open and afraid. Then they left.

The young people felt that it had been a great victory, and they praised the Lord. They thanked the Lord for giving them words that were effective and without argument. And they thanked Him for the sense of love they each felt in their hearts for these poor people. The chants that evening were either subdued or nonexistent. Across the street I listened for them, but did not hear them.

It had been a long and arduous weekend — both for us and the cult. We appreciated Elijah on Mt. Carmel as we never had before, and knew what missionaries meant when they spoke of a "power encounter." We had been through one — not with human beings, but with forces opposed to the God of the Bible — and God had won. We prayed that all those leaving this campus, going back across the country, would at least this once have to recognize that there is a God in heaven (Daniel 2:28), that no other god can do what this One does (Daniel 3:29) and that He alone is the God of all the kingdoms of the earth (2 Kings 19:15).

20

SUMMER 1977
"BARRELS OF WATER"
(I Kings 18:33)

We had known from the beginning that God had placed us on this campus along with the spiritist cult in order to show forth His glory. Dr. Alan Tippett, a missionary friend and fellow professor, often spoke of the tremendous witness that can result from a "power encounter" such as Elijah faced on Mt. Carmel (1 Kings 18). There was not the least question in our minds that we were in the middle of a power encounter.

Along about May or June another aspect of the story of Elijah began to impress itself upon some of us. That was those barrels of water. There were four of them, then four more, and again another four — twelve in all that were poured over the sacrifice. Elijah wanted no question at all that there had been any trickery, or

HELP THIS BOOK HAVE SEVEN LIVES

LEND THIS BOOK TO SEVEN OF YOUR FRIENDS

1. Name: _____
    Comments: _____
    _____

2. Name: _____
    Comments: _____
    _____

3. Name: _____
    Comments: _____
    _____

4. Name: _____
    Comments: _____
    _____

5. Name: _____
    Comments: _____
    _____

6. Name: _____
    Comments: _____
    _____

7. Name: _____
    Comments: _____
    _____

any solution other than God's power which would light that sacrifice. The wood was not only thoroughly wet, but the trench around it was filled to the brim. In no way could an accidental spark from somewhere ignite the wood.

For ten years we had lived and worked among Mayan Indians in Western Guatemala. At 8,800 feet, it was cold. I did every bit of work I could possibly do seated in front of our only source of heat, a wood-burning fireplace in the living room of our home. There was rarely an evening throughout the year when I didn't have a fire burning.

I loved the wood fireplace except when we returned to Guatemala from our furloughs in the States. Then there would naturally be no pile of previously dried wood, and the spark just wouldn't catch. I could buy wood fairly easily and cheaply, but it took months to really dry it out, especially during the six months of the year when it rained every day. And what a frustrating experience to try to light a fire in the fireplace when the wood was "wet."

And there was Elijah, soaking that wood with barrel after barrel of water!

During those months after we got our option to buy the campus, we also had our barrels of water which God poured over our sacrifice. We also had to come to the place that, humanly speaking, there was absolutely no way we could meet that October 1st deadline payment.

For two years I had had a large lump about the size of an egg on my right arm. Two doctors had said it was probably O.K. — "just don't bother it unless it starts to grow."

"Roberta, I think your lump is getting bigger," Ralph said to me in March.

"Oh, surely not," I answered, but for the thousandth time I measured it with my left hand, and looked at it in the mirror and wondered: "What if . . .? Oh, Lord, not now . . . please, not now. If it is cancerous, what will Ralph do without me? Only Prudence will be left. Can he bear the agony plus fulfill your call? And where will we get the money for surgery?"

And again, for the thousandth time I committed it to the Lord, and went on about my business.

In March Ralph and I were asked to take part in a student missionary conference at Westmont College in Santa Barbara, the first they had had in five years. We were to stay in the president's home. Dave, Ralph's brother, had been the president for only one year, and his children greeted us happily as we rang the doorbell of their lovely home.

But Dave and Diane were gone to a meeting of the presidents of all the Christian colleges, and Diane's mother had come to be with the children. "Oh, dear," I thought.

We had lived overseas most of the time since Dave had married, and after returning to the States had seen them only occasionally when they visited from Michigan or Spokane, Washington. Diane's mother I knew casually, but certainly not well enough to drop in on her, mercies of the Lord — and we found them to be oh, so tender.

But the stress of all this was the first barrel of water over the sacrifice.

————

Time was passing fast. Ralph was working night and day to line up consultants and a board of reference. "If we don't have people who are well known willing to stand behind us, then we can't even begin to raise the money," he kept saying. Friends would ask, "How much money have you raised?" and he would answer, "None. We're still lining up the consultants." As May wore on, that answer became more and more embarrassing.

But more and more top men in the field continued to respond: "I'll be honored to be a consultant. I think it is a great work you're doing there. Please keep me informed." And the list rose from 5 to 10, to 20, 30, and 40 — all choice people. Likewise those he asked to serve on the Board of Reference also responded positively.

Now, at last, in June, having used up eight precious weeks and with only four months left until our payment was due, we could hold our heads up in public and start raising funds.

For weeks Ralph had been trying to reach Bob Schuler of the Garden Grove Community Church. "He is interested in missions. He has a television program where he can appeal to Christians. Maybe, just maybe he will help us."

But we couldn't even get to him. He was out

of the country. That was our second barrel of water.

Then Ralph tried to contact Channel 40, a Christian television station. The brother-in-law of one of our interested college students was high up in the staff there, we were told. Maybe they would help.

But again, no response. Another barrel.

We heard that several had recommended us to the 700 club in Virginia — a program on another Christian television station. And a month or so later we heard that again we had been recommended. We received a questionnaire to fill out — then silence.

"Have we heard from the 700 Club?" Bob asked me as we passed in the corridor.

"No. I guess that must be another barrel. God just isn't letting us rely on any human help, it seems." I thought about the cattle on a thousand hills, and all the silver and gold, and oil, that belong to the Lord, but I couldn't imagine how some of that would land in our bank account at the Center.

We were working madly on a colored brochure. All the experts from other mission agencies insisted that the first thing we needed was a nice brochure, and our volunteer help had written and rewritten, sketched and resketched, planned and replanned. The graphics department was about to go crazy with the constant redoing. Ralph wanted a famous personality for the front cover. He is himself fairly well known in mission circles, but not far beyond that. We didn't have the nerve to ask Billy Graham. Maybe Corrie Ten Boom would be willing?

She probably would have been, but her board wouldn't let her even see our letter. "She is already far over-extended," they explained. "She's such a soft touch; she wants to help in every Christian endeavor."

About that time the sacrifice seemed really drenched — at least to us. But God said, "No, pour on more water."

"Maybe now it's time we try some professional fund raisers," some of our staff suggested along in July. "Here we are just a few weeks away, and we have barely raised any money at all. It's too bad if we have to give them a third of what we raise, but they really know what they're doing, and we'll come out ahead. Anyhow, it's the only chance we have."

Ralph didn't want to seem stupid, or obstinate, or know-it-all, so he agreed to talk to some. One man who was highly recommended to us had raised millions of dollars for a Christian project in the Northwest. He was interested in what we wanted to do, but no, thanks, he had too many jobs already. As he put it, "You don't even have a mailing list."

Then we talked to another, recommended by a Christian organization, and another recommended as having raised millions for a project in the Midwest, and another. Always the answer was the same, "There just isn't enough time to raise that kind of money." One came to see us on his own initiative, and promised the sky, and we thought, "Maybe this is God's answer." But things didn't fit together, and again God shut the door, hard! Another barrel!

So we were on our own. No, we were thrown back totally on God. Darwin Hood, a brilliant young Christian realtor, had been watching this going on, and because we had no professional fund raisers, left his job and joined our staff.

We were stirring up a lot of dust, but seemingly not accomplishing very much. Our volunteers were working day and night, setting up businessmen's luncheons, calling churches to set up presentations, completing the brochure. But having no mailing list to speak of, we were starting from scratch.

"How about a promotional movie?" someone suggested, so Ray Carlson of International Films, one of our member organizations, made one in one week flat.

Or how about asking the other now-well-off Christian organizations to help us? Or how about contacting foundations? We had high hopes that several would come across with $100,000 apiece. If one small church can do that, can't a wealthy foundation or organization? Or maybe some godly millionaire (and we knew there are quite a few) would want a building named for his mother? Or how about . . .?

How our heads spun with the possibilities. And how our hearts danced in joyful faith that God would work his miracle that way.

But it was not to be. And that was another barrel of water, and another, and another. Mr.

A was out of the country. Mr. B had already committed all of his money. Mr. C didn't believe in giving money to buildings. *X* foundation had lost a lot of money through an unfortunate, unavoidable circumstance. *Y* Foundation might help us next year, but now now. *Z* Foundation wouldn't even listen to our cry for help. Everywhere we turned trying to "hook a big fish" we caught nothing. Absolutely nothing!

"God, what are you doing?"

———

It was near the end of July by now. We had the magnificent example of $100,000 promised by that small church in Portland and pledges of $1000 each from several college students, but not much more. We needed $850,000 to even go into escrow on October 1, and we would lose a significant part of that if by the next April we didn't have another $650,000. We were thus convinced that to be safe we should do our very best to raise the entire $1.5 million, or get it in sight, by October 1st.

Surely by now that sacrifice on the altar was wet enough to prove that only God working miracles would suffice. When would the fire begin to fall? Even the newspapers in their articles about the race between us and Summit said how wonderful the Summit people were, and had very little to say about us except what the Summit people had told them.

And about that time there fell what seemed to me the final blow.

"Mommie, the doctor thinks I have tuberculosis."

It was like a thunderclap. Ralph was in India, speaking at a conference and helping to set up the South India Center for World Mission, to be a sister center to our own. Linda, our third daughter, had been working at the Center all summer, and part-time during the previous year. She was now returning to college full time, and had had chest X-rays taken to fulfill a routine requirement for entrance. She had been the first college student to donate $1000 out of her hard-earned savings for the Center property. And now this.

"How on earth could you have gotten tuberculosis? Do you have a bad cough?" I hadn't noticed anything unusual. "Are you running a temperature of any sort? Do you perspire at night?" I went through all the symptoms I could remember in my frantic state. "Why does he think you have tuberculosis?"

"I had to have X-rays, and he says . . . he says . . . there is a spot on my left lung." Her voice broke.

We were talking over the phone, and I could visualize her in tears, and they started running down my face also. "Oh, Linda, surely not." And I breathed, "Oh Lord, have we not had enough?"

"This also is in my hands," I sensed Him say, and my spirit quieted.

"O.K. Lord, if it is in your hands, then you will take care of it. Just make us able for the test."

Was this another trick of Satan to stop us? He wasn't giving up easily, there was no question about that. And I reminded Satan again that Christ had once and for all gained the victory, that he had no power over us at all except as Christ allowed it. That we belonged to Christ.

Linda went on. "Mommie, I have to go back for a lot more tests tomorrow." Again her voice broke.

"That's O.K., honey," I said, "I'll go with you." And I prayed with her over the phone, and we committed her to God.

It was a rather restless night for both of us, constantly awakening, constantly pleading with God, constantly recommitting.

Linda had been born in Costa Rica, and at five months had moved with us to Guatemala. In the Indian tribe where we worked there was a great deal of tuberlosis, and we had all the family innoculated with BCG, even though U.S. doctors felt it to be of no value at all. As an infant she had been carried on the back of the girl who helped me in the kitchen, but this girl was very clean and healthy, and I couldn't understand how Linda could have gotten tuberculosis from her.

But I remembered also how repeatedly I would catch her at age 3 or 4 playing with the Indian children, and as children do, eating off the same apple, or some such thing. She might have contracted it then.

Or did she work too hard her first year in college, when she would arise at 4:30 in the morning and walk through the snow at Wheaton to work in the dining hall. Or had she worked too hard this last year?

The doctor must have taken twenty X-rays, and I worried a bit about the amount of exposure she was getting, knowing that cancer specialists warn against too many X-rays. I saw four of the films when the nurse placed them on the lighted wall for the specialist to examine. There was absolutely no doubt about it. She had a spot about the size of the end of my little finger in her upper left lung.

"Oh, Lord. Please take care. With Ralph still in India, I can't even talk to him about it. Please, Lord, take care." And again that certain peace came.

That was certainly another barrel of water on the sacrifice. Even the trench seemed full.

"Mother, he says it's all sealed off. I must have had TB when I was a child, and you didn't know it. But it's O.K. now. I have to take care of myself, and not be around anyone with the disease, but I can go on to school."

Again the Lord had answered prayer, even before we knew enough to ask. How I praised Him!

Barrels of water! Of what value were they to us? Satan meant them for our harm, but the Lord used them to strengthen our faith, to let us know that we could depend on Him and on Him alone. He was sufficient.

And then the fire started to fall.

21

AUGUST 1, 1977
AN UNEXPECTED SPARK

"Would $50,000 help?"

Hal Leaman gasped, then said, "It certainly would. Who is this calling, please?"

"Howard Ahmanson."

Two weeks before on Friday night Beth and Brad had gone to a seminar in Newport Beach. Chuck Miller, the leader, had married them a year and a half before, and both of them had tremendous respect for his leadership in discipling. At the seminar they had been separated into small groups, each group studying the Bible in Chuck's unique, fresh way. As the weekend progressed, they became well acquainted with the others in their small groups. Beth was in Howie Ahmanson's.

"Ahmanson, Ahmanson . . .," she said to herself when first introduced. "Where have I heard that name before?" But she just didn't connect this young, obviously brilliant young man in a Bible study setting with the Ahmanson Music Center in downtown Los Angeles, or with Home Savings and Loan.

Howard had become a Christian the year his father died and he became one of the trustees of the Ahmanson Foundation. It was a heavy burden for a young person still in college to carry.

In the course of the evening on Friday someone in their small group had asked Beth what she was doing, and a brief summary of the story of the U.S. Center for World Mission spilled out—all about the 2.4 billions of beyond-the-range people, the spiritual struggle with Summit, the desperate need for money, and the great challenge should we succeed.

In the later, larger meeting Chuck echoed some of her words, speaking on the tremendous need and the fantastic opportunities, should God so ordain.

Howie called us on a Monday. He could promise $50,000, he said, and could hope for $100,000 more. He couldn't have known it, but his gift was the beginning of a great groundswell of interest and response on the part of all sorts of people, none trustees of foundations, but many matching him in excitement about God's concerns. And his gift buoyed up our faith when we most needed it.

"Yes, $50,000 would certainly help."

22

AUGUST 29, 1977
"NOT MANY MIGHTY"
(I Corinthians 1:26)

We were really counting on foundations. We had been told repeatedly that it was impossible to raise big money in a short time without receiving a number of very large gifts from foundations or wealthy people. "All the Christian nonprofit organizations depend on these foundations," the authorities insisted.

It was hard enough, being novices, to find out whom to approach. It was harder yet to approach them. Clarence Church of the Wycliffe Bible Translators told us, "You have to write a good proposal to present to the foundations. That is a specialized kind of job which requires a lot of skill and costs several hundreds of dollars. But we believe in you. We will arrange for one of our proposal writers to do one for you."

The resulting proposal was good. It was professional. We were proud of it and very grateful. Ralph took it with him along with a notebook full of background data when he went to Dallas. But the various foundation heads only glanced at the material, and started firing questions. That didn't bother Ralph. What would have troubled him is if they hadn't bothered to ask any questions. Some of them seemed really interested.

Back home we prayed, "Surely, O Lord, this is the way you will answer our need. These people have money to give to your cause. We need that money which belongs to you, and *we need it in two weeks time* or we will lose the campus to those who will lead people away from you. What are you going to do about it?"

The foundations didn't turn us down — exactly. They just didn't pick us up. Maybe it was the suddenness of the whole idea. Maybe it was the time of year. Certainly it was not God's plan for that first payment — because the money didn't come, not that way! The only Christian foundation that helped us was the Billy Graham-related foundation. One Christian foundation told us, "If Billy Graham's foundation gives, we will also." Billy Graham did; the other didn't!

Evidently God didn't want this campus to be bought with the money of a few wealthy individuals. Could He get more glory out of the sacrificial giving of college students, missionaries, unsalaried people, and ordinary laymen from all sorts of backgrounds and from all kinds of churches? I was often reminded of the verse which said, "Not many wise, not many mighty . . ." because college students, working part-time to pay their way through college would send in $1000, or a girl who would be a bride in a few weeks gave her wedding money, or missionaries gave their entire savings accounts. Yet there were some who could easily give $1000 who gave $15 while those precious students, many of them, gave $1000. One girl sold her car, and is traveling by bus to work now. People from very modest homes in the neighborhood around us walked into the office with $100, $200, and $500 checks.

What really was hardest for me to accept was when our staff who worked for us all summer without pay gave what little they had in their savings accounts saying, "The Lord has provided for us thus far in a miraculous way. Surely we can trust Him to continue."

We presented programs in local churches, and were grateful for their gifts. Two, both in Portland, Oregon, matched those students in their unusual and amazing generosity. One was Bethlehem, Gene Davis's church, with its pledge of $100,000. The other was Aloha.

Aloha was almost like a sister church to Bethlehem, also Baptist. Some of its members had heard Ralph speak at a banquet sponsored by the Bethlehem church. They wanted their church to get in on the blessing of proving what God can do for those who truly trust Him, and asked Ralph to speak at their church on a Sunday morning near the end of August.

"I don't know how to tell you this," Ralph was greeted when he arrived at the Portland airport. There was a pause.

"Yes?"

"Well, our church burned down last night. Someone set fire to it, and the main sanctuary burned completely down. We have a suspicion that it may be somehow connected to the public stance the church has taken against allowing homosexuals to teach in our schools. This is the sixth church in this area to have had a mysterious fire in the last few months, and almost all of these were active in that vote.

"What should I say in a situation like this?" Ralph thought. "I can still talk about missions and about the 2.4 billion who need to hear, but how can I ask these people for money to help us get that campus so we can reach the unreached? They are going to have to rebuild. They will not be building to have greater or nicer facilities. They have to build in order to have a roof over their heads. What can I say?"

But he spoke at both services the next morning in a large room in the education building where they met for worship. After the service the pastor and elders met to discuss what the church should do about its building and also about the challenge Ralph had presented to them.

Later that evening Ralph heard an amazing report:

"We believe the Lord wants us to tithe our insurance adjustment on the fire," they told him. "We hope that will bring you about $50,000, but it may not all come in at once. Then maybe we can bring it up to $100,000 like the Bethlehem church. We will do our best."

23

JULY 23-28, 1977
PETE AUSTIN

"Ralph, this man is asking questions I've never heard before."

John Patterson, the young, ever-smiling realtor from Portland, seemed momentarily stopped in his tracks. It was toward the end of July. A few weeks previous Dr. Gene Davis had called saying that John was dropping his own business for a couple of months in order to help us. He would be driving down with his wife and two babies. Could we use him?

Could we ever! John was the kind of person you couldn't help but love. Not long a Christian, he had an exuberant faith — in fact just couldn't understand how things could ever be anything but "up!" He had grown up in Tennessee, and seemed just the man we needed to talk to church leaders, businessmen and foundations in the South. No sooner had his family settled into an apartment near the Center when John was off, flying to Florida and Atlanta and Tennessee. Jack McAlister of World Literature Crusade had offered to pay his transportation. Now he met Ralph in Wheaton, Illinois, there for the National Conference of the Association of Church Missions Committees where Ralph was to give the concluding address.

John was referring to Pete Austin III, an engineer from Chattanooga and chairman of the missions committee in the large First Presbyterian Church where Ben Haden is the pastor. John was supposed to have the answers to the questions when he ate breakfast the next morning with Pete, also in Wheaton for the conference.

"You know, Ralph, Pete is nobody's fool. He's really brilliant! He's in the business of developing properties, especially shopping centers. If anyone has tough questions, he's the one!"

John paused and looked quizzically at Ralph. It wasn't hard to see that John was wondering if even Ralph could answer those questions.

"He wants to know the price per square foot of the campus, the replacement value, our pay-off schedule, our ratio of indebtedness. Have we had the property appraised ourselves?" John went on and on.

"Just a minute, John. Let's sit down and work this out. I believe we have the data we need — I worked it out some time ago, in fact," Ralph assured him.

John, like many others, had forgotten that Ralph was *not* just a professor. He also was an engineer. He knew accounting and business matters, and what he didn't know he could find out. Mathematics had been his way of relaxing ever since Caltech days.

Even though Ralph had a talk to give the next day, John had to be ready for Pete, so they stayed up late, going over Pete's questions one by one and working out the answers.

"Ralph, I wish you could come to breakfast with us," John said wearily about midnight.

"I wish I could, but I had another appointment even before I got here. Don't worry, John, you've got all the data you need. Those are solid figures. And the Lord will be with you."

Later in the day when Ralph saw John, he was all smiles. "We had all the answers. I think he was really impressed!"

Pete Austin had been so thorough in his investigation that from then on if we had any tough businessman asking those kinds of questions, we told him to call Pete. Furthermore, Pete went home to Chattanooga and convinced the missions committee at his church.

Out in Pasadena we on the staff laughed when Pete reported to Ralph, "You can imagine the raised eyebrows in session when our committee requested $25,000 for you. 'We've never given that much to any cause! And for bricks and mortar in California?'"

We knew the feeling. But Pete had immense

prestige in that elite circle of bankers, lawyers and professional men.

"I could have pushed it through," he told Ralph, "but I had a better idea. I suggested they ask you to come and answer their questions!"

"Maybe he thinks if I can answer his I can answer anybody's," Ralph laughed as he told us he was leaving.

There were sixty men and women there. Their attitude was friendly but some of their questions were tough. Back and forth, one after another, and then Ralph dropped the bomb!

"Just this past week we decided we shouldn't accept any money from any missions committee. We feel that the Lord wants this campus bought in $15 donations from a million people. We know we can't reach a million people overnight, and therefore are willing to accept larger gifts temporarily. But when large gifts are eventually replaced by $15 gifts we intend to ask your church whether you wish us to return or reassign these funds for overseas use."

The people looked at each other in disbelief. Was this Winter guy out of his mind? Nobody, *nobody* ever gave money *back* to a missions committee. What would they do with it?

"Don't worry! There's plenty of need," Ralph assured them. "We just want it to be very clear to everyone that we are not trying to divert any mission money. We may need whatever you can give us to meet our deadline and to acquire the property, but we're determined to give it back just as soon as possible."

It wasn't easy to explain why we had felt led to this small gift approach. It was not a gimmick; we simply didn't want churches and mission agencies to be afraid of us nor to feel we were launching any major competition. We were out to serve them, not to become a mission agency ourselves. Furthermore, we were convinced that unless one million people were to gain a brand new vision about the "hidden" or the unreached people and become what we called "World Christians," the Center had no future anyway. Thus stressing $15 gifts would force us somehow to reach a million people with new vision.

But could we?

24

AUGUST AND SEPTEMBER, 1977
MAIL TIME

Every day now the stack of mail was larger. And every day almost every letter that came in carried a check. Some days the total was $1,000, or $5,000, or $10,000, or $20,000. Two missionary families gave $10,000 each. The Lord was answering prayer. But would we have enough soon enough?

Ralph couldn't follow in detail the amount of money that came in, nor the types of people who were giving. But he was greatly encouraged that instead of a few very, very large gifts, we were getting hundreds of $50 and $100 gifts from people of modest means. To him this meant that Christians at the grass-roots were with us.

And they were. We had gifts from Nazarenes, Baptists, Presbyterians, Episcopalians,

Lutherans, Methodists, Pentecostals, Independent church people, people in the Midwest, in the Northeast, in the South, in the Northwest, in the Southwest. We still do not know how so many people heard about our need in so many different places. There is no way we can explain it but that God prepared the hearts of His people all over the country, in all walks of life and from all churches to reach out to answer His concern for those we are trying to reach. Some people read about us in the newspapers, in articles that sometimes were slanted against us, and sent in money because they recognized the spiritual battle we were facing. A man 3000 miles away, not a Christian, wrote to us because he knew the battle we faced with Summit.

It was exciting to be the receptionist those days. She was the one who got to open the letters and sort them out.

Not all the communication with the Christian public was by mail. We had to install five additional phones to handle the calls that were going in and out, and asked our staff to stagger their work hours so that the phones would be covered from 6 AM until 10 PM daily. Even Saturdays and Sundays the last few weeks we had someone take calls because people who had been praying for us called and wanted to know how things were going. Those were exciting days.

25

AUGUST 18, 1977
MERCEDES

"Roberta," Mercedes said to me one Monday noon in early August. "What do you think of the idea of a benefit concert?"

"Well, I've never in my life thought one minute about such a thing. The whole idea is totally foreign to me. But I'm game. Why not?"

Every Monday each of the thirty-some organizations which formed the U.S. Center for World Mission sent a representative to an Interfacing Meeting. One Monday the Fellowship of World Christians would report, telling how many college students were now taking our *Understanding World Evangelization* Course, or how many fellowship groups around the country were meeting regularly for study and prayer for missions, or what students on which campuses were planning a Student Conference on World

Evangelization (SCOWE). The next week International Films might be the reporting organization, or the Fellowship of Artists in Cultural Evangelism, or the business office of *Missiology: An International Review*. This day it was the turn of Providence Mission Homes, an organization started in 1974 by Jacquet and Mercedes Gribble to provide housing for furloughed missionaries. They had become involved in this campus even before Erik Stadell, since at that time they had bought the college's 24-unit apartment house for married students and turned it into missionary housing. That building was only three blocks away.

We had known Mercedes for years. She had been Dr. Paul Rees's efficient secretary when he was a pastor in Minneapolis. Now she was even more busy locating homes, cleaning apartments, finding furniture and kitchen supplies — anything that any missionary (or national pastor) on furlough might need.

But she was not only a servant of the Lord. She was also a woman of great faith!

"I have a friend who is the sister-in-law of Norma Zimmer's pianist. She thinks we might persuade Norma to put on a benefit concert for us. The Providence Mission Homes could sponsor it, and the proceeds would go to help buy the campus. Norma, you know, sings on the Lawrence Welk show and often sings at Billy Graham crusades. People always love to hear her. What do you think?"

Again I said, "Why not? Let's try it."

But when Mercedes called, Norma said that she would have loved to come, but, alas, her schedule was absolutely filled for nine months ahead. By that time Mercedes had already booked the Pasadena Civic Auditorium for one of the two nights it was still free in September — the fifteenth. Now she would have to cancel the booking.

Meanwhile, eight new missionary families had come for the fall term at Fuller, and Mercedes had to clean apartments and find homes and furniture for them. "Perhaps it's best to forget the whole idea," she said, quite discouraged.

But she didn't cancel the booking at the Civic Center.

26

AUGUST 22, 1977
"YE HAVE NOT
BECAUSE YE ASK NOT"
(James 4:2)

To those of us seated in the office, the suggestion should have seemed ridiculous. After all, a person as famous as Pat Boone must get a lot of money for a concert. He wouldn't do one for us free!

By August, however, the Lord had performed so many miracles for us that it seemed only natural to ask for one more. There had been the miracle of space on a campus almost totally leased out to an Eastern religious group. And the miracle of rent far less expensive than we could hope for. And the miracle of the $15,000 option for an $8.5 million campus. The miracle of competent and dedicated staff coming out of nowhere to volunteer their time. A first-class promotional movie made in one week flat, 43 top missions executives willing to work with us on an unprecedented idea out of the blue, etc., etc. The Lord had been so good to us. And he had commanded us in the Bible (Psalms 78:32) to believe him for even more.

And we did.

Ralph had an idea. "I have a good friend who is a good friend of Pat's. Maybe he can intercede with him for us."

"But you haven't even seen Vernon Grose since Beth got married," I interposed. "He doesn't even know that you're no longer at the seminary. Just to fill him in on all that's going on will take forever."

"It's not that hard. Let's try it."

But Grose was out of town, on vacation with his family. We knew that his hometown was Spokane, Washington, so Ralph called him there.

"They just left for home."

"Are they coming directly back?" Ralph asked.

"I think they're stopping off for a few days in San Francisco. But if he calls here, I'll tell him you're trying to reach him.

Was the Lord saying "No" or "Just wait"? We didn't know. But we had to wait, no matter what, so we did.

"Hello, Ralph. I hear you've been trying to reach me. What can I do for you?" Vern said when he called toward the end of August.

"Man, is it ever good to hear your voice!

We've been trying for weeks, it seems, to reach you."

"So I hear. How is everything?"

The two had become friends some years previously when Vern had been working on the problem of the teaching of evolution in the schools. Both were members of the American Scientific Affiliation, an organization of Christians with scientific training. Ralph had at that time pointed out to Vern that the "continuous creation of matter" was a concept well known and widely discussed among scientists. Couldn't Vern build on that fact in his argument for at least a reference in school texts to the Biblical story of creation?

Now maybe Vern could help us.

"Hey, man. Have you heard anything about what I'm involved in? You know that I left my job at the seminary last October, don't you?"

"No, I hadn't heard that."

"I've been writing for some years now about the 2.4 billion people in the world who are beyond present outreach, and finally I felt God wanted me to do more than just write about it. So the long and the short of it is that a group of us are trying to buy the former Pasadena (Nazarene) College campus to set up a major mission center whose only purpose is to focus attention on those 2.4 billion people." He went on to explain in greater detail about the challenge, the competition with Summit, the financial need, and, at last, his purpose in calling.

"I know that people are all the time asking Pat Boone for favors. But if we could just get him to give us a benefit performance, that would really put us on the map as far as Christians in this area are concerned. Now, I don't know just how much he knows about missions, or if he is even interested in them, but what do you think?"

"Well, Ralph, you know Pat usually gets about $20,000 for a performance. But I'll ask him. He's a great, spirit-filled Christian. I know he is interested in the Great Commission, and he just may do it for you."

The next day Vern called Mercedes. When he explained his mission, she was both astounded and embarrassed — astounded because no one thought we might get Pat Boone and on such short notice, and embarrassed because through some slip-up Ralph hadn't been informed that she had assumed there no longer would be any concert.

"Mercedes, Ralph asked me to see if Pat Boone could help you. Would you like me to call him? I know him quite well."

Mercedes thought fast. She had been headed in one direction, then had been forced to turn around. Now should she, could she, turn back around? Was there time for that? Surely the Lord would provide someone to help her.

"Yes, I would appreciate it if you would call him. We still have the auditorium booked for September 15th, but I don't see how we can manage to put together a program that fast. I know that the Civic is also available on the 24th.

Would you see if Pat will be in town that night and if so, if he would be willing to do a benefit performance for us then?"

So Vern called Jan, Pat's secretary, and found that the 24th was in fact the only night Pat could possibly come. Mercedes took it from there and called Jan, who said, "Will you send a letter to Mr. Boone telling just what you want of him?" She had seen, she said, our "hidden peoples" ad in *Christianity Today* and a couple of small news items about our Center.

I don't know whether the Lord graciously delayed the arrivals of a few missionary families so that Mercedes could have time to write that letter, but by the next morning she was in Pat's office with the letter and some literature about the Center.

27

SEPTEMBER 1, 1977
ONE QUESTION

"There is just one question Mr. Boone has," his secretary said over the phone to Mercedes that afternoon when she called back. "Is the project likely to succeed?"

All sorts of people have been wondering that. Anybody watching the Children of Israel, right out of slavery, start across the desert toward Canaan would have asked the same question. Watching them again as they crossed the Jordan and headed toward Jericho, they must have asked it again. Jericho was one of the major cities of that time, heavily fortified, its walls extremely high and thick. And who on earth were these "slaves", out to do battle with this?

Who were we? Nobodies, really. Ralph was known in the world of missions, but no one on the staff was widely known. We were very much like the Children of Israel, out to do great feats with nothing to guarantee success but the confidence that God wanted it done. One thing we did know. Any success we might have could not have come from us. We were all absolute novices. There was not a single person on our staff that had ever raised any funds, printed any brochures, made any movies, put on any fund-raising dinners, designed any spot announcements for radio or TV, planned any concerts. We were absolute novices — *ab-so-lute!*

"Did we have a chance to succeed?" Well, whom was he asking? Us, or God? "With God all things are possible to him who believes." But all things don't always work out, that we well knew. It was already the first of September. We could not get by with less than $850,000 by October 1st, and we had, in hand, only $47,000. We had another $232,000 pledged, but together that made only $279,000. Did we have a chance?

Mercedes took a deep breath and said, "Yes." And that was it.

28

SEPTEMBER 2, 1977
PAT BOONE

"Dave, there's a call for you on line two," Gwen, our receptionist said.

"Hello. This is David Bliss speaking. May I help you?"

"This is Pat Boone's office calling. Mr. Boone would like to speak with you."

"Pat Boone speaking. About that benefit performance. My secretary tells me that you can get the Civic Auditorium on the night of the 24th of September. That just happens to be the only even partially free night I have in September. My daughter is having an open house, and I had planned to go, but perhaps I can arrive late. What I'm saying is that I'll be glad to help you."

"Praise the Lord! Thank you. You'll never know just how much this is an answer to prayer."

"Now in a performance of this kind I usually do one or two light numbers that people probably expect from some movie I've done, and then I move into something more spiritual and give my testimony. Most of the program, of course, will be in your hands."

"Yes . . . well, we'll have to talk about that. Would you mind if I got Dr. Winter on the phone? I want you to know him and a little bit more about this vision. I don't know if Vernon Grose told you much about him and this project, but I think it will help for you to talk to him."

"That's fine. Go ahead."

So Ralph and Dave talked to Pat Boone for an hour or more. They talked about our dream here on this campus, about the needy world, 84% of which no one was even trying to reach because they were "hidden" people behind cultural and prejudice barriers that Christians couldn't (or wouldn't) cross. Yet God wanted them saved, and Christ would not return until they had had a chance to hear.

"Was Pat interested in missions?" Ralph had asked Vernon Grose. He found that he was, very much so, and that he was a member of the governing board of several mission societies. He listened attentively, asked keen questions, seemed genuinely concerned. Ralph was really impressed.

A few days later Ralph, Dave, Mercedes and Nancy DeMoss were seated in Pat's office, high above Sunset Strip. Thirty minutes before, Dave had roughed out a possible program for the concert. He was embarrassed to show it to Pat's agent because it was so amateurish.

"How did I ever get into this mess?" Dave asked himself. "Why was I fool enough to think that since I had helped put on a Paul Stookey concert I could undertake this with only three weeks lead time? That's almost like saying I'm qualified to be the president of the country because I once shook hands with the President."

But there was no one else who knew any more than he did, David realized. True, David had once been responsible for ticket sales for a promotion dinner for Chuck Colson, and he had helped in the organization of a Leighton Ford crusade on Cape Cod, but that was all. It was as if the Center leadership had said, "We can do it; now YOU do it!" And that was it. So here he was.

He held his breath. He fully expected Pat's agent to say, "But this is crazy. This will never work." Instead he said, "I think this will do."

After that initial conversation with Pat on the phone, Ralph and Dave had rather boldly said that what they had in mind was a bit different from what Pat had in mind. Pat had suggested that he sing a few songs, give his testimony and go. Dave suggested something far more.

"We were thinking of you as more or less the moderator, or the master of ceremonies. Ted Engstrom will be there to spell you off, but this is not the usual audience. These will all be a special kind of Christian, people interested in missions. You don't have to start where you usually do."

"Um, I see. You want me to really move into the concept of serving God and of reaching out to the unsaved. You want me to have the world in mind, not just the unsaved here. And you want me to more or less emcee the whole thing. Well, O.K., I'll do it."

Wow! What a man! And what a God we all serve!

"Pat would you also be willing to give us a radio spot? I have a rough one written out here for you. Would you be willing to look at it?

"Sure, fine."

Equipment was brought in and it was done right then and there. There was, again, a great feeling of oneness in the Spirit as they planned together. Pat himself closed the meeting with prayer. And then they left.

"Roberta," Ralph said to me later, "Pat is a genuine Christian. He is real. There was not a thing about him which I would have wished to find which I did not find. He is a man of God."

We had hoped for a Christian celebrity. We got instead a man filled with the Holy Spirit who was highly interested in missions, willing to serve in any way he could to help that cause, and a warm brother in Christ. We knew that he was exactly the one God had chosen for us for that night. Neither of us dreamed then that he would be involved with us even beyond that program.

29

SEPTEMBER 6-20, 1977
A WILD TWO WEEKS

It was the day after Labor Day, and it was wild around the office. We now knew Pat Boone would give a concert for us, and even though we were all total amateurs, we knew putting on a concert involved a lot of work. David Bliss was named the person in charge.

David had come to us in July from Gordon-Conwell Seminary in Massachussetts where he had been the head of the fast-growing student missions group. He had inherited from his father, on the pastoral staff of the famed Park Street Congregational Church of Boston, a certain dynamic personality to which people responded. He was a leader.

But he had no staff.

"Let's see. The concert is on the 24th. This is Tuesday the 6th. That gives us exactly 18 days to get ready," and he mopped his brow. "How can I, alone, ever do it?"

But who could help?

Hal Leaman had gone back to Boston that first week in September to raise funds on the East Coast. He would be gone the entire month. Ralph was absolutely swamped with work, far behind in urgent correspondence as well as speaking here and there and contacting churches and foundations by phone. David Welch, our volunteer from Cincinnati, was frantically calling all over the country, trying to set up more contacts for Ralph or for John Patterson. Brad was arranging speak-team presentations in local churches, as well as organizing the Sunday "Jericho marches." Bob Coleman and Dave Cashin were writing news releases, others were answering phones, sending out letters, doing accounts, writing articles for magazines and arranging open-house meetings. Darwin, a graduate of the college and a local realtor, dropped in "to help" and ended up sending letters all over the country to college alumni as well as helping first one David then another with their monumental tasks.

We were all very tired and terribly busy.

And then the day after Labor Day the Lord sent Mildred Rylander to us. "I have a thirty-day vacation," she said as she walked into Dave's office, "and I wondered if you could use any help?"

"Could I ever!" David exclaimed as he looked up at this obviously competent woman. "I don't even know where to begin, and we have to put on a concert in a little over two weeks."

"What we need to do," Mildred said, as she set down her purse and prepared for work, "is to decide each morning what we have to finish by the end of that day in order to be ready on time. Now, what about today?"

And they went to work.

Walking by their office I could see Mildred seated by the telephone with large stacks of directories beside her, calling printer after printer, or artist after artist. Any volunteer who happened to drop by was snagged to run errands of all sorts.

They started immediately on posters. Mildred called someone she knew who was a professional, and asked if he would donate some time. She called Pat Boone's office, requesting a photograph for the poster, then called Wes Crist, a volunteer, to go and pick it up. She called a man who owed her a favor, and asked that he produce our tickets by that weekend. He did! She called someone she knew who specialized in programs, and arranged for him to design a cover and begin the process of printing the program.

David Bliss, meanwhile, was also on the phone: to Leighton Ford, "Will you give us a testimonial?" To Dr. Harold Ockenga, president of Gordon-Conwell Seminary and well-known evangelical leader, "Will you call Billy Graham for us and ask him to call us the night of the concert?" To Eldridge Cleaver, in San Francisco, "Would you come down to see what we're up to and say a few words for our program on the 24th?"

No one turned him down.

By this time Darwin had moved completely into David Bliss's sphere of activity. When Eldridge Cleaver arrived on the 21st he showed him around the campus and discussed our goals and vision with him. He asked him about his own experiences in countries almost "closed" to the Gospel. And all this time they were being recorded.

It was quite a wild two weeks. Clearly God was working miracles all the time.

30

SEPTEMBER 12, 1977
NANCY DeMOSS

Nancy DeMoss is a most unusual 19-year old.
I first learned about her through an article in
Eternity magazine. "What a gal," I thought to
myself. "Here she is, still in college and yet the
department head over the entire primary Sunday
School of one of the largest Sunday schools in
the country." She was a senior at the University
of Southern California, majoring in music, and,
I found out, a concert pianist. "Wow!"

Through the years Ralph had bumped into
her uncle Robert, who heads up Partnership in
Mission, an organization which is developing
overseas initiative in mission causes. Ralph had
heard her father, Art DeMoss, speak of his own
conversion and had been profoundly impressed
when he had said, "Only once in my life did
anyone ever invite me to accept Christ, and that
one time, I did. What if no one had ever asked

me?" Art had gone on to tell of an occasion when he had been rooming in Mexico City with a high official from Israel, and had pressed him to consider whether Jesus was not, in fact, the Messiah.

"You don't understand," the ambassador had insisted. "I can't accept Jesus as the Messiah. I have 64 relatives here in Mexico. I just can't do it."

But in the middle of the night Art awakened to this man's screams of, "O.K., I surrender!"

And he became a believer, and won eleven more of his family in the next two weeks.

This was Nancy's family — a dynamically evangelistic father, an uncle whose whole heart was in missions, and, apparently a number of younger brothers and sisters and a mother who are enthusiastically behind them.

Mercedes had gone shopping that morning, the Pat Boone concert very much on her mind. "What can we have on the program besides Pat Boone? He wants a 'back-up' group. It would be asking too much to have him sing the whole evening," she thought. At the store she "happened" to meet one of her friends from church and mentioned our dilemma.

"Maybe I have an answer," that friend responded. "How about Nancy DeMoss. She is young, attractive, and really sold on missions. Moreover, she is a concert pianist. That might be just the right touch."

"Hmmm . . ." Mercedes said. "How do we get in touch with her?"

David was delighted. "That's just right! When can I hear her play?" He knew that she would have to be good, really good, to share the platform with Pat.

She was! Moreover, she had arranged for her own enjoyment a Great Commission medley consisting of beautifully arranged hymns combined with talking, and ending with the words "If you know it, why don't you share it?" Dave thought it was perfect. An additional plus is that Pat knew her family, had been in her home and she in his. They knew and respected each other already.

Dave came back to the office entirely satisfied and brought with him not only Nancy, but her father who was visiting from Philadelphia.

It was obvious that Nancy was her father's daughter. They had the same dark, piercing eyes, the same infectious smile, the same self-confident yet humble attitude. I liked them both immediately.

Art DeMoss asked us all about the Center, why we wanted to buy it, what it cost, and how much property was included. And Nancy wanted to know about the 2.4 billion unreached people. "Could you give me some literature to take with me?" she asked, as they were leaving. At first I thought that besides all her other talents, maybe she was also very courteous. Then I realized that she was genuinely interested. "I am a speed reader, and if Dad doesn't have time to read it all, I can fill him in," she said. "I really miss being able to discuss missions with my Uncle Bob."

31

SEPTEMBER 6-24, 1977
BEHIND THE SCENES

We were all novices, but God had many servants in the Pasadena area who were real professionals, willing to help us free or at minimum cost. On looking back, we shudder to think what might have happened without them.

David Bliss and David Welch had taken it upon themselves to organize a prayer council of Christian lay people in the area. They met each Tuesday night and prayed for the Center, for the concert, for fund-raising efforts, and for the by-now extremely weary staff. Their prayer buoyed us up during the day, and no doubt protected us from the darts of Satan that were headed our way.

That prayer council also brought much-needed professional hel. On Thursday the 16th Dave talked long distance to Leighton Ford, Billy Graham's brother-in-law, taping what he said on Ralph's secretary's dictaphone. The transcription when amplified was terrible.

"How can we use this at the concert?" Dave asked Ralph in despair. "It's just awful. Somehow we've got to find better equipment." And he dashed off to try out first one person's transcribing equipment, then another's. On Tuesday night the problem was still so much on his mind that he asked for prayer at the prayer council meeting.

"Why, that's easy," Dick Marsh said. "I can help you on that!" Dick, we learned, was the vice president of a chain of radio stations. He had heard about the prayer council at his daughter's birthday party. Elizabeth Curtis, a well-known realtor in Pasadena, a Christian and an alumnus of the college, had attended, and there spoke about the Center, urging people to pray for us.

"That's not our only problem," David continued. "Our Pat Boone radio spot is too long, and for the life of me I can't figure out how to cut it."

"Listen, you just come over to my office in Arcadia after hours and I'll get someone to help you," Marsh said.

It was after five when they left for the radio station. David groaned when he saw the rush-hour traffic, and wondered if they should have started an hour sooner. Being new to the area, he had visions of having to drive twenty or thirty miles.

"Where on earth is Arcadia?" he asked Darwin, seated beside him.

"Oh, it's about ten minutes from here, about as close as you can get."

"Well, praise the Lord for that."

The following Tuesday, around noon, Jamie, our new receptionist, a volunteer sent down by the Aloha Church in Portland, took a long distance phone call for David. As she had been instructed, she asked, "May I ask who is calling, please?" then nearly dropped the phone.

"Billy Graham."

At that very moment David was talking to Pat Boone's agent. It was a rather awkward situation.

"Mr. Henley, there is only one person I would pre-empt you for, and that is Billy Graham. Well, Billy Graham is on the other line. Can I call you back?"

Billy apologized for calling so close to our deadline for the concert. He said, "I have just come back from the campaign in Hungary, and I have a thousand letters on my desk and 250 phone calls to make. I just wanted to get through to you people right away and help you in any way I can."

Billy called back to the studio the next day where they were ready to tape his message. It was not his words for the concert audience that heartened us most. It was his genuine interest in what we were attempting. "How are things coming? What is the other group's progress? How much have you received? How much do you need? I'm sure we can help some."

32

SEPTEMBER 17-24, 1977
MISSIONS MULTI-MEDIA

The date of the concert was fast approaching. We had 30 minutes of recorded tape from Eldridge Cleaver, another 10 from Billy Graham, and about 10 to 15 from Leighton Ford. We had alloted only 6 minutes of program time for all three. Darwin and Ken Johnson of Mr. Marsh's staff worked for hours to shorten those tapes, splicing, cutting, rearranging. Darwin assembled slides of each person to show on a screen while his recorded message would be played.

Saturday night, the 17th, David Bliss and Ralph decided that, contrary to what they had previously planned, our promotional movie just wasn't right to use in that concert setting. Something else had to be done. After Pat Boone, anybody would be anticlimactic except Billy Graham or Jimmy Carter, and unfortunately, they weren't available! That we knew without asking. Dave wanted some sort of audio-visual, but to produce that could take weeks. And the program night was exactly one week away.

Mildred knew another professional, a neighbor of hers who was a Christian and an audio-visual specialist. Maybe he could help. "The trouble is," she said, "Ken Dymmel is just out of the hospital after having a heart attack. The last thing in the world he needs right now is a rush job."

And everyone who had ever done a multi-media production said there just wasn't time enough. "It's impossible." Everyone, that is, except Ken Dymmel and Dick Marsh and Ken Johnson. They all said, "We can do it."

"But I've got to have the script by Monday morning, without fail," Dymmel warned.

It was now 10 P.M. Saturday, and Dave was extremely weary. He had felt he was an amateur about everything else he had been doing, but he knew a good deal about multi-media productions. He had done some really professional presentations before, enough to know it was a lot of work. "And, I suppose," he said to himself, "I am the one, therefore, who will have to write that script." He was so very weary, but if it had to be done, it had to be done.

Briefly he jotted down a rough outline of what he wanted. By this time in September, our nights were like days, and the offices were almost as fully staffed at 10 P.M. as they were at 9 in the morning. Thus, when Bob came walking by,

Dave called him in, showed him his outline and asked him to fill it out a bit, if he could. "You're in the writing department, Bob. We have to have this script by Monday. Do you think you could flesh it out for me? I just have to go home and get some rest."

Bob had been working night and day on the script for a proposal to send to secular foundations asking for their help. But he dropped that momentarily. Dave didn't know that Bob had had some multi-media experience himself, having done several productions, the latest just three months before. And Bob had a nearly incomparable grasp of our message.

So Bob sat down and went to work, joined soon by Darwin who returned from supper and a brief rest. "Call me when you're ready to have my input," David said as he left.

It was around midnight. Dave woke from a sound sleep and grabbed the phone. Sarah, their three-year-old, was a sound sleeper, but he didn't want to risk her awakening.

"Dave, we're ready," Darwin greeted him.

"Well, I'm not. Listen guys, I'm really shot. Do you think you can carry on? I can look at it tomorrow afternoon, but right now I'm worth absolutely nothing."

"O.K., no sweat." And they went back to work. They worked all night and in the morning, bleary-eyed, they showed it to David.

"That's great. That's really great. How'd you guys do it?" David asked.

Ken Dymmel liked it, too. He had a few slides that would work, Bob had a number that would do, they took a few more pictures, and they borrowed three from an organization nearby that "never, under any circumstances whatsoever, loaned out originals" — but did!

They still needed a narrator. Dymmel knew Phil Read, a Nazarene CBS announcer who, he thought, might do it for us. And he did, beautifully!

We had a great multi-media program, put together by all sorts of God's servants at almost no cost to us. It was ready on time, and had only one or two near misses. But that is another story.

33

SEPTEMBER 20, 1977
GETTING THE WORD OUT

Dave was really pleased. Everything was moving along fine. True, Bob working on the multi-media presentation had already lost two nights of sleep and would probably lose more before Saturday; we still had a stack of posters to distribute; ticket sales weren't as fast and furious as we had hoped — but things were falling into place.

"Could you fix us two large flower arrangements for the platform?" Mildred asked Phyllis, a local florist.

"I'll be glad to. Moreover, I'll donate them if you mention my name on the program."

"How about ribbon bows for separating the different sections of the auditorium?" Mercedes mentioned to a friend, and found that this friend already had just what we needed.

The problem of offering cups was more difficult. Mercedes and Jac scoured the city the day of the concert and bought all the large popcorn cups they could find. Still lacking at least a hundred they approached a local theater manager, who said, "Sure, I'll let you have all you want, so long as you buy them filled with popcorn. That will be 75¢ each."

"No thanks," they said, and we made do with what we had.

Some ideas we had were good, some bad. The spot on the radio was producing numerous phone calls now, and several of the local Christian bookstores which were selling our tickets called for more. We tried putting flyers on all the cars with Christian bumper stickers, but didn't find as many as we had hoped. Perhaps all the Christians were home and in bed by 9 PM but we doubted that. But we didn't find them, and we ended up with a thousand flyers that were unused.

"Do you people need money, by any chance?" different ones of us were asked from time to time. That question always stunned us. Here we were, sinking or swimming, and people were asking if perchance we needed a rope to help us out. How could they have missed our cries of "HELP"?

"We'll just have to do one more thing," David Bliss said on Tuesday morning. "What we need is a big, half-page ad in the Star-News, say, a letter from a well-known local pastor and carrying endorsements from a number of the leading citizens of Pasadena. I wonder if Pastor Raymond Ortlund of the Lake Avenue Congregational Church would be willing to sign that letter?"

"He'll never do it," his secretary said. "Ray has a policy to never do anything like that. I wouldn't even bother to ask him."

Dave persisted. "Ray has known Ralph since seminary days. He believes in him and in what he does. Ralph grew up in this church. Why don't we at least let him see a letter I've prepared?"

"He's not here. He's at a pastor's conference about sixty miles away. If you think it's worth a try to drive that far, you may, but I think you're wasting your time."

For weeks we had wondered just what Ray Ortlund thought of what was going on with us. We knew he had been in England for a month-long conference. We knew also that the type of confrontation we had had with the cult was not the sort of thing that he might like to get involved in as pastor of the largest church in town. And yet the previous Sunday he had led our Jericho march with Ralph. True, he had been embarrassed and reluctant at first, but that evening he was bubbling from the experience.

"Will he, or will he not? That is the question," we thought. Was it worth our time to pursue?

"Hey, I'll be glad to," Ray said when he saw the letter. And we were off on another orgy of phone calls, asking first one Christian citizen and then another to endorse that letter with Ray. Few turned us down.

"Oh, it's too bad that ad is tucked way back here with the comics," I said to Ralph when I saw it Friday morning. But look at all those signatures — forty-three of them."

"Why, that's where I look first, don't you?" many told us.

34

SEPTEMBER 20-24, 1977
LAST MINUTE FRENZY

"Do you think we can pull them both off successfully?"

Saturday was the night of the big concert. Sunday afternoon was to be our final, triumphant (we hoped!) Jericho march.

David Bliss, in his great need for help with the concert, had appropriated staff all over the place, so Prudence almost singlehandedly had to plan the march. She called the police for permission to use the streets, then decided against it. (We used the sidewalks.) She planned refreshments, then decided that, having no idea how many would show up, she'd better just make it punch. She frantically searched for trumpeters, hoping for ten, and finding, at last, three. She organized and directed a choir composed of our staff.

"Prudence's second name should be 'Patience' or 'Grace,'" I said to Ralph. "She certainly gets enough tribulation to produce either." Her name had quieted a troubled sea on one occasion when an irate man had called, complaining about what the newspaper had said that we had said (and hadn't).

"What is your name?" he had at long last asked her.

"Prudence," she answered.

"What does that mean?" His voice took on a quieter quality.

"Wisdom," she said.

And the name fit her beautifully. She was a strong source of steadiness and wisdom in those days of hurry and frustration. Her office was continually occupied by someone who needed her quietness in order to go out and face the fray again. She was a gift of God to us.

Thursday night, before the concert on Saturday, Ralph and David Bliss decided we should film the concert and the march for future use. The initial payment of $850,000 would only take us into escrow. We would need $650,000 to get us out of escrow, and then another $13.5 million to complete the purchase of the campus and the 84 off-campus houses, which we would also need eventually and which would be permanently lost to us if we didn't get them now. We had counted on 3 million of that for endowment, to be augmented by the rental on the houses. Businessmen who looked the plan over had thought it a sound one. Yet we knew that publicity would be important to us for a long time to come. We had just begun to fight.

David Cashin was put in charge of contacting the film people, arranging the details with them, and helping with the job itself. In a word, David was given general directions, and then left to his own creativity. No one had time to do more. And no one needed to do more.

Friday night, one night before the concert, Ralph and Darwin, David Bliss and David Welch had another late meeting, quite by accident.

"We really need something to break up the opening songs. Some little something that will set the tone for our emphasis on the unreached peoples of the world. What can we do?" Ralph asked.

"Hey, how about a skit? We could have three foreign students from the three large blocs of unreached peoples — the Hindus, the Muslims and the Chinese — and have someone ask them a few questions," Bliss suggested.

It was about midnight when they finished, and somehow David Cashin again got the ball thrown to him. He worked for an hour or so on the script, and went to bed.

"Dave, you have a good tenor voice. Can't you help in the choir for the march? Christy and I are growling well out of our range, trying to help the two tenors out, but my voice is really getting strained. I don't think we can do it."

I had walked across the front hall where we were practicing that Saturday morning into the front offices, where I had found David pecking away at a typewriter. I knew nothing about the late-evening consultation. I didn't realize that David was working on a skit for that night — a skit which wasn't quite written, had no actors, and had no stage planning to back it up.

"What are you doing?" I asked him, as I looked over his shoulder.

"Say, I'm really in a jam. I've got to find some foreign students before ten, and it's nine-thirty already."

I could see that his typing was rather slow, that he seemed a bit harried, and I foolishly thought that if I helped him out, maybe he could help me. So I typed, rewrote some sections, and retyped, while he made phone call after phone call, netting nothing.

"What's this for?" I asked.

"It's a skit for tonight. It comes on right after Pat Boone's first song. And I have to get someone from India, from China and from the Middle East to help. No one seems to be in at the seminary."

"Look, I'm finished now. Why don't you take these pages with you and drive over there? Quite often students are wandering around the grounds or are studying in the library." I was reminded of Jesus' instruction to "go out and compel them to come in."

Somewhere on the way, Dave decided that rather than depend on memorized parts, he would have these three (if he could find them) read their scripts from behind the curtains while just in front another group of three would be silhouetted by a soft blue light from behind.

That meant getting three more men, and for these we drafted any man of near-right size and shape who happened to come near the Center before noontime.

It was now two in the afternoon. Beth and Brad were already at the auditorium, selling tickets for the concert. David Welch was there also, helping the prop men set the stage. Darwin and David Bliss were making last-minute checks, arranging for left-over tickets to be picked up, phoning here and there, seeing that the on-stage phone was installed. They were doing so many things that they themselves were dizzy trying to remember it all later. Bob was in Ken Dymmel's office, putting slides in the carousels for the multi-media presentation.

Before that first meeting in Pat Boone's office, David Bliss had written a tentative production script to be followed the night of the concert. It detailed minute by minute who would be doing what on stage, where they would stand, where to enter and exit, when the curtains would be open or closed, what spotlight would be where, when, when the house lights would be darkened for the media show — in short, all the various details necessary for a smooth performance. That initial script had by now been rewritten at least ten times.

Now, at 4 PM on the day of the concert, David Bliss called all those present at the civic auditorium to meet together and go over the script one last time. Somehow it didn't seem quite right to him, but he couldn't lay his finger on just why.

"Would you guys pray with me? I feel so pressured. This script just isn't coming together right. Let's ask the Lord for guidance."

It was a time when all hearts were warmed by the Holy Spirit, and all bodies relaxed once again in His care. They came out of that session, went over the script once more, smoothed out the rough spots with ease now, and rushed off to find a typewriter. There was an old one in the room next to the ticket booth, and David started to use it.

"Say, wouldn't that be easier with an electric typewriter?"

It was the manager of the civic auditorium who had just walked in.

"It sure would."

"Follow me. We have a good one upstairs."

They not only had an electric typewriter, they also had a Xerox machine, and in a few minutes David had the 15 copies he needed for Pat Boone, the various participants in the program, and for the stage, light and camera crews. God had even taken care of that.

35

SATURDAY
SEPTEMBER 24, 1977
H-HOUR

"Doc, can you do these introductions in the skit? I called Dr. —— but he said he just didn't have the time to prepare for it."

It was after 6:30 PM, the very night of the performance. We had gone to the auditorium a bit early to see if we could help anywhere. The script for the Unreached People's Skit was thrust into Ralph's hands, he glanced at it and made a few hurried changes. Finding his "actor-readers," the foreign students Dave Cashin had rounded up earlier, Ralph checked their parts with them, again made a few changes, tried to memorize the few lines he would have to do without script in front of the curtain, and that was it. The program was about to begin.

"Lord, you know we want this program to glorify you. We have worked as hard as we could, but we have had so very little time. Now it's in your hands. You will have to put it all together," they prayed silently. Out in front the rest of the staff greeted friends, passed out programs, and also prayed.

Only those close to the situation realized just how much God had been working to put it all together, and how much He would still have to do. Bob, inserting the slides into their carousels an hour earlier had suddenly realized that he was missing one complete set, left by accident at the photo studio 8 miles away. His car had been malfunctioning lately, and he hoped and prayed it would get him there before the lab closed.

Dave Cashin had turned from the Unreached Peoples Skit to his other task of helping with the filming of the program. The film crew was all in place, except for the sound man who had not arrived as yet. Someone would have to double for him a the beginning, and Dave grabbed Ken Ekstrom, a Caltech student, and one of our summer workers, who was just passing by.

David Bliss and Darwin were all over the place. The people out in front were getting restless because the doors hadn't opened yet. And Pat Boone still hadn't arrived.

By 7:15 people were filing into the auditorium, chattering excitedly among themselves.

"What is that tract they're passing out in front?" my sister asked me as she stopped by for a moment.

"What tract?"

"Well, I guess there are really two of them. I

just glanced at one. It seems a bit wierd."

"Oh, no!" I thought, and edged my way out to see.

Out on the sidewalk in front, two people, one on each side of the front steps, were busily handing out literature. I got one of each item and looked them over. One was obviously put out by a semi-Christian cult in the area (not Summit), and the other was put out by its detractors, also a bit off base as far as evangelical Christians were concerned. Neither had anything to do with us or the Center.

"What should we do?" I asked Mercedes.

But there was nothing we could do. These people were on public sidewalks, everyone on the staff inside was much too busy to do anything about it, and we decided to commit the situation to the Lord and trust that our guests would be able to figure it all out.

It was now nearing 7:30 and people were taking their seats. The flowers were in place in front of the curtains, the ticket lines beginning to dwindle in the front hall.

At 7:30, the time the program was to begin, Bob dashed in with the missing slides just ahead of Pat Boone. He began the long climb up the twenty-foot ladder to the 2½ by 2½-foot platform where he was to sit to show the multimedia and wondered if he could stay awake. He had had no sleep the night before.

"We have no one to cue us when to shift from one camera to another," Fred Roberts whispered to Dave Cashin, out in front in the orchestra pit. "Can you do that?"

"What next?" Dave thought to himself. "I've never done it, but I've never done all sorts of things I'm having to do. Why not?"

"Just tell me how. What are the signals you use?" he asked Fred.

36

7:30 P.M.
SEPTEMBER 24, 1977
THE CURTAIN OPENS

"Pat's here. We can begin." Excited whispers circulated back stage. "They want us all to meet for a few minutes of prayer before the curtains open."

And then they were on.

"He looks so young, so vibrant," I whispered to my daughter beside me. "Maybe it's that white suit and forest-green shirt. I know his daughters are all nearly grown so he has to be almost forty."

From the very beginning the songs were Christ-centered, speaking of God's love for each of us and for all mankind. Ralph is usually not very emotional, but when Pat sang "Jesus Loves the Little Children, all the Children of the World," tears came to his eyes. It was in every way a concert — Pat and Nancy DeMoss were both excellent — but it was much more than that. In front of me were Presbyterians, beside me two retired missionaries of the Church of the Nazarene, on the other side young people from the Lake Avenue Congregational Church, and behind, other youth from the Glendale Foursquare Church. We were Methodists, Baptists, Catholics, Episcopalians, yet we were all no more than brothers and sisters together who dearly loved our Lord.

"Do you suppose there are any Summit people here?" I whispered to my daughter Becky.

"Back to the left there are a few," she said. "It must be an eye-opener to them to see so many different kinds of Christians fellowshipping so joyfully together."

The curtain closed, and Ralph stepped out, the spotlight on him.

"Good evening, I am Ralph Winter, and I would like to introduce to you three friends of mine whom you have never met." Then turning to the first of the dark silhouettes to his right, he went on, "Friend, where are you from?"

There were three of them, one from India, one from Asia and one from the Middle East. In each case the Gospel had come to their part of the world but had not reached them, they pointed out.

"Why?" Ralph wanted to know. And the Chinese (from a voice behind the curtain) spoke of the Communist persecution and said that to his knowledge he had never seen a Christian.

"There are Christians in my country," stated the Hindu, "but they are almost all from what was formerly called the outcaste group. We of the castes admire what Christ has done for them, but we will lose all our family and friends if we join with these people."

"We," said the Muslim, "believe that Jesus was a prophet, but most of our educated youth today look to science to solve our problems."

Dave Cashin, in the orchestra pit, was having problems. The sound man had arrived a few minutes after the program had started, and to his horror Dave realized that he was hard-of-hearing. "Somehow I will have to relay my signals to him by a tap on his arm, or something," he said to himself.

Behind the back drop, high on the platform, Bob had just slipped his final slide into place. Maybe now he could breathe easily for a few moments.

37

SEPTEMBER 24, 1977
GOD PUT IT TOGETHER

"Pat who?"

The audience was rocked with laughter. This was the third try on a long distance line in the middle of our Pat Boone benefit concert. The first two tries had produced nothing but "I'm sorry; you have reached a disconnected number." We had checked everything out ahead of time, explaining to Dr. Ockenga, president of Gordon-Conwell Seminary near Boston, that we would be calling. What was wrong now?

"Dial *one* first." someone shouted from the audience.

Now at last the phone was ringing, as the entire audience could hear.

"Good evening, Dr. Ockenga. This is Ted Engstrom at the Pasadena Civic Auditorium. We are having a benefit concert here this evening for the United States Center for World Mission, and I have Pat Boone standing right here beside me. Would you like to say hello to him?"

Later we wondered if the line had been bad and Dr. Ockenga hadn't heard his name, or if Pat Boone somehow just wasn't in his repertoire of entertainers. But for Californians, his question brought down the house.

Pat was smooth. At one point the curtain caught a microphone and started to throw it to the floor. Pat casually stepped to the right, reached out, deftly caught the mike, and continued without missing a beat. He had only glanced at the program script as he walked onstage, but every song was in place, every person introduced properly and ever transition exactly right. Even when the curtain opened once when it was supposed to be closed, he cooly carried on.

Nancy also was great. She looked tiny and beautiful in her long black dress, but she played with precision and great competence. She was the perfect performer to share the stage with Pat. "I've been in her home, and she's been in mine," Pat said as he introduced her. Both were so obviously at ease, and both obviously loved the same Lord and loved doing this program for His glory.

Each time the curtain opened and closed, the basket of flowers on the right of the platform turned a little as it was brushed by the curtain. Mercedes, seated in the front row was madly trying to figure out how she could get word to someone backstage to move it out from the curtain before it tumbled over completely. But she was at a real loss. So the flowers kept turning back and forth as the curtains opened and closed.

It was now time for the multi-media. The house lights were dimmed and the screen lit.

"I wonder how this will go," Bob thought as they turned on the various projectors. "If only we could have gone through this just once." Ken Dymmel, on the same high platform a few inches away, was thinking the same thing, and committed the show to the Lord.

Seated halfway back in the audience, I was very pleased at how well-organized the media show was. Just the right pictures and words. The slides faded into the motion picture portion and back again, one slide slipping slightly at one point.

Out in front we didn't know the half of what was going on high up on that platform backstage. The movie projector had started to smoke, and Bob was furiously blowing on it to keep the film from burning. By the time the slide projector clicked in again, its light burning in his eyes, Bob had become quite faint from hyperventilation, and losing his balance, almost fell the twenty feet from the platform. Out in front we saw only the slipped slide.

That was the way the evening went. To those of us in the audience it seemed a beautiful, well-organized performance. Backstage, only God held it together. Not one of us could doubt that this was another of His miracles.

38

SEPTEMBER 25, 1977
THE JERICHO MARCHES

There were three loud blasts of the trumphets, immediately followed by "Hallelujah, Praise the Lord" shouted by the hundred marchers who followed them. Farther back a second group of a hundred took up the refrain, "For He has done great and mighty things." Back and around the corner, the third group echoed, "We will praise His name for ever and ever." And the first of two interspersed choirs began to sing.

It was the seventh and last of our Jericho marches. Six Sundays before we had been a band of about fifty who gathered to pray in silence as we marched the one and a half miles around the campus we were claiming for God. Today we numbered 350, including three trumpeters, two banner-bearers, ten ministers, two choirs and the three praise groups of over 100 each. Because we had to march two-by-two on the sidewalk, the group stretched for blocks, never in a straight line, as it wound its way around the campus.

The six previous Sundays had been without incident. Only a few people noticed us, and in cosmopolitan Southern California, those few had not bothered to find out what was going on. When Ralph first suggested that we march around the campus, there was almost no one on the staff who wanted to do it with him — it was too bizarre. "This isn't Jericho, after all. God hasn't commanded *us* to do that," they reminded him.

Some were quite adamant. "Do we really want to seem like kooks? Is that the message we want to give the community?"

It was true. God had not commanded us, and Ralph didn't really know why we should do it. He just felt that by this means we would announce to the world that we were claiming this campus for God and for His cause. "There is something about a public witness that is good for us as well as for the community," he said to me.

Even I had qualms at first, but not for long. On that first march in August I prayed as I walked, and as I prayed I wondered if the Children of Israel hadn't felt a bit odd, not fighting, as they were prepared to do, but just walking. How the people of Jericho must have leaned over the walls and sneered at them, "Do you think you can capture a city that way? How stupid can you be!" And it must have taken courage to be willing to seem stupid.

A newly-arrived member of our staff had, at our suggestion, visited the Summit campus bookstore and bought a tape made by Elizabeth Clare Prophet. On this tape, amidst her leading decrees and chants, she had spoken about Joshua and the city of Jericho. She had made some comment about how ridiculous it would seem if anyone were to do that type of thing today.

"I really believe we should do it," Ralph repeated when hearing this. "Those who really don't want to go with me don't have to, but those who do, let us do it in confidence and faith."

So we did. Actually, though, Ralph was out of the country for the first three marches, and Hal Leaman, as Associate General Director, led us. With him that first Sunday was Bob Pierce, the founder of World Vision. We will probably never know how hard it was for Bob to make that march. The doctor had told him that he was slowly dying of leukemia. He had been in bed off and on for extended periods of time, but always refused to stay there, instead visiting mission stations all around the world, and raising money to help with the immediate needs he saw.

"Ralph, I'll be glad to march with you. I am leaving Sunday evening for the East and then on to Irian Jaya, but I don't want to miss this. Of course I'll have to cancel the meeting I have with Billy Graham at his home in Montreat, but I'm sure he will understand," Bob said.

So here he was, in the hot sun of August,

walking that mile and a half with us. He was flushed when we got back, and I worried that we had asked too much of him.

"I came to this campus as a 12-year-old boy," he told us afterward, "and stayed here until I was 20. I went through high school right over there in a little building across the street, now replaced by that nicer one. Miss Mayfield, our principal, was one of the godliest women I have ever known. As we walked around the campus I recognized house after house as having belonged to one or another of my professors at the college. I used to walk home almost daily with old Uncle Buddy Robinson or talk with Dr. Wiley, the president for so many years, there by that fountain in the front of the school. This campus has belonged to the Lord since just after the turn of the century. We cannot allow the devil to claim it now."

I also had walked this campus as a student not quite so long ago. I could remember some of the saints of which Bob had spoken, now all of them with the Lord. And I also prayed, "O Lord, this is hallowed ground. It was used from its beginning as a college to send people around the world proclaiming your gospel. While seated in the branches of one of these trees, Esther Carson Winans determined to give her life as a witness to the Indians of Peru. In that auditorium hundreds have knelt at the altar, asking you to fill them with your Spirit that they might go forth to serve. Will you allow pagan gods to desecrate this holy ground? Won't you take possession of this Canaan again?"

"Do not let this small beginning be despised," Bob Pierce urged us. "All great things started small, and if God is in it, as I believe with all my heart, it will succeed."

The next-to-the-last Sunday was a glorious day. Pastor Ortlund from the Lake Avenue Congregational Church had joined us with a number of his parishoners, so we had almost 200. Some of our people from the Center had smiled at his slight hesitation when he informed the church congregation that morning that he was going to march, and invited others to march with him. We could remember our own mixed feelings five weeks before. But by now we were "old hands." We were not surprised when that evening he reported to his congregation: "I went on that "Jericho march" this afternoon with the staff of the Center for World Mission. Wow! What a blessing! Did you ever miss God's moving if you weren't there. It wasn't just the 200 or so who marched. I could just sense the presence of the Lord Himself with us. I felt almost like I was actually with those Children of Israel when they marched around Jericho. Wow!"

During that last week before the seventh Sunday I worried some. "You can probably count on 50," Satan would remind me. "Those are the old faithful. But after last Sunday you are really going to look like losers. Pastor Ortlund will be gone, and all his people probably won't come back. You thought you could get a great group, but you'll never make it."

"It is your name at stake, Lord Jesus," I

reminded Christ when I prayed. "We've been willing to seem foolish for your sake. But now you have to bring in the people to help us."

Prudence was having a hard time finding trumpets. Then one day Mrs. Fischer, who had prayed for my tumor, called and said that her son played the trumpet, and wanted to help. Would we call him?

This was the son who had himself been healed of cancer so many years before. He not only came with his trumpet, but brought two other trumpeters the banner, and entire church choir with him. With them, our old faithfuls, and others who came after first hearing of the marches at the Pat Boone Concert, we had seven times what we had started with seven Sundays previous. How could we get more Biblical than 7 times and 7 Sundays?

Now it was September 25th. This Sunday we had to circle the campus seven times. Our initial payment was due October 1st and we still had a total of $157,000 in the bank and an additional $222,000 in pledges out of the minimum needed of $850,000. We would truly have to march the victory march "by faith." As 50 of us circled the campus six times silently before the final triumphant march, we remembered God's words, "not by might, nor by power but by my Spirit, says the Lord." (Zech. 4:6) We knew we had no power in ourselves. We also knew that God loves to use the weak to confound the mighty, that all He needs is people who will let Him use them. So we marched in faith and in prayer.

The first, second, and third marches on that last Sunday were uneventful, except that for the sake of time we had to move so fast. Several marchers developed blisters and had to drop out, only to be replaced by others. As mile after mile was traversed the silence began to build our hearts to a great anticipation. We didn't know how God was going to work, but we did know He was going to do something great.

All the previous Sundays the Summit people had almost totally ignored our marches except for broadcasting classical or Christmas music (in August!) on their loudspeaker as we approached the front of the campus. This Sunday, by the time we were completing the fourth march, some of them gathered on the lawn in front and watched. We wondered what they were thinking. And we prayed for them as we marched.

Two small boys, doubtless members of the Summit community, started down the hill on their skateboards heading for the line of march, going faster and faster, only to finally swerve away when the march continued step after step toward them. A couple of marchers were splattered with raw eggs from a dormitory window on the Summit campus. But mostly it was a silent, inexorable marching to the final and last triumph. As we rounded the back of our building after each circuit, people gathering for the final march would questioningly hold up fingers, asking in effect, "Which round is this? How many more times to go?" Even one Summit person on the other side of the campus asked, "How many times have you gone around now?" And he breathed a sigh of relief when the person at the end of the line held up six fingers. Returning to our patio to line up for the last march, the crowd of 250 gathered there greeted the somewhat weary earlier marchers with a burst of applause.

Prudence had spent days deciding on the sequence of the last march. Unlike the Children of Israel, we had no "fighting men." Our soldiers were the "praise troops." But like them we were led by the trumpets, then came the banner and the ten ministers (like Joshua's priests) followed by Praise Troop I, Choir I, Praise Troop II, Choir II, and Praise Troop III. Only the choirs were supposed to sing lest we get out of tune and meter with each other, strung out along the mile loop as we were. But as we rounded that last corner on that last march and the Choir began to sing "Jesus, Jesus, Jesus, O there's something about that name," all of us spontaneously burst into song. To the Summit people Jesus was only one of a number of ascended masters. To us He was Lord of Lords, and King of Kings — the One at whose Name one day every knee shall bow and every tongue shall confess that He is God, the only one worthy to receive the power, the riches, the wisdom, the strength, and the honor and the glory and the blessing (Rev. 5:12).

What a day! What an experience!

But the end was not yet!

39

SEPTEMBER 26 - OCTOBER 1, 1977
D-DAY

"Praise the Lord!"

Jamie, usually rather quiet, picked up the stack of mail she had just opened and headed upstairs to the accounting office.

"Do you know how much came in today?" she asked Mary Fran as she passed her desk. "Twenty-seven thousand dollars! Just look at that stack. Most of it is in checks of $100 or less. People all over are responding to our need. The Lord is really answering prayer!"

I had been praying for some time now: "God, does it have to be a last minute miracle? You know I hate cliff hangers. Can't you do it this once ahead of time?"

And He had, part of it!

Several college students had given $1000 apiece — money hard earned to pay for their fall tuition. Two missionary families had given life savings. For the last two weeks widows, retired people, people with little money had walked into our office and emptied their checking accounts.

Ralph had urged people to call us that last week to find out how we were doing, and our lines were very busy. Billy Graham called with a pledge of $10,000; World Vision called and later hand delivered $25,000; Gospel Light Press brought in $10,000, Providence Mission Homes gave the $26,000 earned from the Pat Boone concert.

But we still lacked almost $400,000. Did we misunderstand God when we went into this venture? Many friends had told us we had. Yet He had already worked so many miracles and constantly had reassured us.

On Thursday of that week we had a wonderful idea. "Hey, the 1st of October is on a Saturday. Does that mean that the money is to be paid on Monday morning because of the bank holiday?" Those two extra days looked so essential.

But the college lawyer said, "Read your contract again. It says *'Before'* the six months is out, and that is tomorrow. We'll be over in the morning.

"Boy, can't they even give us until 5 o'clock?" I thought rebelliously. But we went to prayer again and cried to the Lord.

And our governing board went into session, and to prayer also. Some weeks before three different sources had offered to advance $100,-000 each. Even with those loans we would still be short, but they would at least bring the total into a reasonable distance of the required amount. We had not asked for those loans. They were all from Christians. Were they, could they be God's provision for us?

The young people on our staff said, "By no means. We have asked God to *give* us the money; now we must trust Him to *give* it, not loan it." Our board prayed and agonized, and then decided that, yes, these were godly men offering the money. They believed in us; we could not disregard their faith. God had placed it upon their hearts to offer these loans. Even though this was not the way we would have preferred that God answer, it was God's provision, and we should accept with thanksgiving.

It had been a real crisis of faith and trust in our leadership. One board member, Jim Montgomery of Overseas Crusades, reachable only by phone, wrote the following day: "While our board-member phone conversation last night was somewhat somber and subdued, I found myself walking and leaping and praising God around the house after I hung up. I trust the narrowness of this victory will not rob us of the joy nor rob God of the glory of what has happened. Satan wanted to keep us from getting the property in the first place; now he will try and rob us of the joy of victory and God of the glory."

But we still didn't have enough! It was pledged, but it wasn't all there. Two large checks were caught in branch banks in San Francisco, and it seemed they would not arrive in time.

The $50,000 Ahmanson check, delivered by mail the week previous, sat in our files, waiting for our IRS non-profit clearance.

Friday the college lawyer and business manager came early. And we were not ready. We had the promised loans, and we had some outstanding promised pledges, but we didn't have the money in hand.

The staff watched soberly as Ralph, Hal Leaman, David Bliss and David Welch crossed the street to the beautiful library building where the negotiations would take place. We couldn't believe God had failed; but we didn't have the money! All we had were empty stomachs from three days of fasting, extremely weary bodies and a flickering faith.

"Oh God, HELP!"

And we went to prayer again. I felt much like the children of Israel must have felt as they faced the Red Sea: "Why, Lord, did you bring us to this difficult place?" We were praying around the circle, and when my time came I could only cry, "Lord, you promised" and then my voice broke, and I fled from the room.

In the library across the street our staff were equally somber, not knowing what to expect. Eric Winter, Ralph's nephew, recently admitted to the California Bar Association, was there as our only legal counsel, and he was firm.

"They received the option agreement two weeks late, and they did not feel they could start raising funds until they had it in hand."

"Yes," they admitted. "That is true. O.K., why not take another week?"

"Praise the Lord," our men breathed silently.

"Also we feel some precise agreement must be reached about the off-campus housing and the Summit lease," Eric continued.

And for two or three hours the discussions continued. What a blessing to be dealing with men of sterling Christian character.

The Lord must have been in that room, for the terms hammered out were in every respect better than we had dared hope. Our end of escrow would now be almost a year away (September 1st, 1978) when Summit would be off campus. Only then would the next $650,000 be due. We could pay a minimal sum for an option to buy the off-campus housing and make the down-payment of $285,000 when we entered escrow for those houses the 1st of October, 1978.

When our contingent returned to our offices and announced the extension of time and the terms of the agreement, we rejoiced, even though we still felt somewhat like prisoners in the dock, awaiting judgment. We still did not have that money we so desperately needed. We had a one-week reprieve.

40

OCTOBER 7, 1977
GOD DID A MIRACLE

All the next week seemed anticlimactic. The huge mail deliveries were now reduced to almost zero. Money trickled in: $100 on Monday, $50 on Tuesday, $30 on Wednesday. The well was dry. From time to time friends would call to ask what had happened, and we would tell of our extension of time and our continuing need and ask them to pray.

Friday morning, October 7th, we were all at the office early. By the time the banks opened David Kolb, our accountant, was at the teller's window. From time to time he had carefully deposited all gifts for the property in a Savings and Loan bank, hoping thereby to gain a few dollars of interest. He now withdrew all but the dollar necessary to maintain the account and drove several blocks away to the bank where we had our checking account. For two weeks we had been expecting two checks from Portland —one a $100,000 loan and the other the insurance tithe from Aloha church. Almost daily David had checked with our bank to see if that money had arrived (We knew by phone that it had been wired.). Each time our bank informed him that unfortunately those checks were still in the branch office in San Francisco.

But today David was really in despair. "What would you suggest we do?" He knew that the bank would not honor that money until it was on the premises in Pasadena.

That was not our only banking frustration that day. Sheri, running back and forth between the office and the bank, reported a new crisis each trip.

"Dr. Winter told David to pass the money withdrawn from savings through the checking account so we'll have a bank record to back up our accounting books. *Now,* just after David finished depositing that money, they informed him that there is a bank policy forbidding large withdrawals less than a week after a large deposit is made."

The next trip: "They can't find that $46,000 deposit I made yesterday at closing time." She was really in a panic over this one.

"Sheri, don't you have your bank deposit book, or a deposit card or an extra copy of the deposit slip to prove you deposited the money?" I asked.

"Oh, yes! Of *course* I do," she beamed, located them and dashed off to the bank again.

Fifteen minutes later she was back again to see if any more money had come in the mail. We had a property deed, given us by John Patterson of Bethlehem, one of our most faithful helpers throughout the summer. It was worth about $11,000, but now we needed cash. "I'm afraid we're going to have to cover that with a loan," Ralph said. "The college authorities may not want to accept a deed." But again, where would we get the money?

"How are you coming? Is all the money in?" It was a man from the area who was calling. Jamie, on the phone, rather discouragedly told him about our deed problem.

"How much is it worth?"

"Eleven thousand, five hundred!"

"Oh, is that all? Well, I can lend you that much for a few days. No problem." And he got in the car, went to his bank, and arrived at our office just in time to catch Sheri on her next flying trip.

All that morning we had been wondering what to do with the Ahmanson check of $50,000. All other large checks had come from organizations having their own tax-exempt status and could be put directly into our own accounting system. But somehow the Ahmanson check needed a tax-exempt receipt which we could give only by giving it first to a sister organization. We had been told long before that it was now much more difficult and could take from six months to two years to get this status. Most people had assumed that only lawyers could properly fill out the forms (for quite a substantial fee). However, the government offices of the IRS in Washington, D.C. had encouraged us to fill them out ourselves. There had been a minor crisis in our office when Ralph had decided to follow the advice of Washington instead of conventional wisdom.

Now it was Friday morning, the 7th of October. We still had not heard from the IRS office. We had little reason to hope we could hear so soon — it had been only six weeks since we had finally filed all the forms. "But we just have to have that $50,000," our accountant told Hal, the associate director.

Ralph had left the morning previous for Columbus, Ohio where he was to address the International Society of Christian Endeavor. This date was beyond our first deadline and had been set for months; it could not now be cancelled. "I'll just have to keep in touch by phone," he said when a number of us expressed dismay that he should be gone during our additional week of crisis.

When Hal explained to him on one of his calls that we didn't know what to do about that $50,000 check, Ralph said, "Have Bruce call the IRS."

Bruce Graham, a meticulous engineer working on our staff, had been the one who completed all the government forms in consultation with Ralph. Better than anyone else he knew what problems we might encounter. He had been in contact with the IRS office from time to time, and had left his phone number so that as soon as our application was approved the person handling our papers could call us, which she promised to do. It was beginning to appear that our papers had been filed too late.

"I'm so glad you called," the girl in the IRS office told him when he called. "We've been trying to reach you, but somehow misplaced your phone number. I just want to tell you that you have your tax-exempt status—on both the U.S. Center for World Mission and the William Carey International University. Congratulations."

We were walking on air when we heard the news. "Thank you, Lord. You've worked another miracle. Tomorrow would have been too late." And Sheri took that check down to David who was at the bank.

David and the bank officials were still in consultation. "We know that $189,000 in the branch bank in San Francisco is on its way. We've talked to our people there, and even though technically we're not supposed to honor that money until it arrives here, we'll make an exception. We know the crisis you're in.

"Now, about the large withdrawal you need to make. That rule is to protect us against questionable deposits, but we know that money is real and we'll let you withdraw it even though you just got through depositing it."

Altogether, scraping up every available penny, we still lacked almost exactly $100,000. Campus Crusade had called earlier that morning having some time before offered a loan of just that much, should we need it. And did we ever! "Someone will have to meet our messenger with the check half-way."

"How about in Pomona?" Hal asked, thinking of the fact that we had to meet the college lawyer there at 5 P.M.

"That's fine."

So David Welch was sent on that trip to Pomona, with instructions to hold the lawyer at his office until Hal could get there with the rest of the money.

Everything was ready now to go, it seemed. Now the bank could write the check for $750,-000 to be added to the money coming from Campus Crusade to make the grand total we needed.

But there was one more slight hurdle. "Our check writing machine can't write checks that large," David Kolb was told. We'll have to give you five smaller checks." And they did.

The rest of the story was one of a mad dash by freeway at the worst hour of the day for freeway travel. Hal arrived a few minutes late, but thanks to David Welch, the lawyer was still there. Papers were signed, and the checks handed over, and they were on their way home.

Ralph had missed the last of that day's excitement, being still in Ohio. He called once more and rejoiced with us that God had truly worked another miracle.

Two weeks before, a long article about Summit in the Pasadena newspaper had spoken of us as "fundamentalists waging a smear campaign against them." The newspaper correspondent, warmly admiring of Elizabeth Clare Prophet, had quoted her as saying, "We want the will of God. If He wants them to get the campus, that's fine."

Those words didn't sound unfriendly. What was unfair and unrealistic were the accusations of "smear campaigns" and the idea of blaming us for the antipathy which the Nazarenes surrounding this campus had had toward their group long before we arrived. These months had been a power encounter — not so much between *us* and *them* as between their "sea of energy" god and ours. They were the ones who from the beginning had had the money; we did not! They had the dedicated followers; we began with only well-wishers. The big difference was the point Mrs. Prophet hinted at unknowingly in her newspaper statement. All the Ascended Masters, Buddhas, Krishnas, and other beings they chanted to so vigorously could not stand up against the power and might of the living God.

God had won a great spiritual victory, and the Summit leadership knew it far more than most Christians in the area. It was clear to all who were willing to see that the God of the Bible, the God who is above all gods had done a great miracle for us. We wanted people to "stand in awe and confess the greatness of the miracles of God" (Ps. 64:9) and to realize that "He does not depend on human weapons to fulfill his plans — he works without regard to human means!..."

(1 Sam.17:47). But even more than for people in the area to confess His miracle working power, we wanted Summit members and non-Christians around the world to recognize Who was speaking when God said, "I am God; there is no other; I have sworn by myself and I will never go back on my word, for it is true — that every knee in all the world shall bow to Me, and every tongue shall swear allegiance to My name (Isa. 45:22-23).

That is the only reason we are fighting the battle we fight!

41

OCTOBER 1977
BRAINSTORMING

"What does God want done in this world? And how can it be done?"

It was a no-holds-barred brainstorming session. Usually only the top staff of an institution are involved in such a heady experience. But our staff was so small and all so totally committed to the vision that Ralph felt all should be involved. "God often reveals His ideas to young people," he quoted Benedict of 1500 years ago. "Perhaps our young staff will be the most important ones to include."

We met for two days in an upper room of our building on campus, praying that God would guide us in our plans. "I want us to think about the whole picture," Ralph said. "We know a good deal about what God *is doing* in our world. We know what He *wants* to do. And we know there is a huge gap between these two. What needs to be done in order for this generation to complete the task of evangelizing the world?"

Those words sounded very familiar to me. How many times in the past, I wondered, have inspired men and women tried to arouse sleeping Christians with that same challenge? It was the watchword of the Student Volunteer Movement almost 100 years before when the Student Conferences for Missions led by John R. Mott and Robert E. Speer, then in their twenties, presented this challenge unequivocally to the youth of our nation. Thousands upon thousands of college students responded. They brought new life to the older mission agencies. They spread around the world, into almost every land, setting up hospitals, schools, agricultural institutions, universities, as well as churches. Back home in the middle of a great awakening our nation became so excited about missions that two presidents of the United States, William McKinley and Theodore Roosevelt, attended missionary conventions and spoke openly of our "mission" to the world as a nation.

In 1906 a small group of former students, now businessmen, met together in prayer for missions and set up the Laymen's Missionary Movement, a movement that would quadruple missions giving in this country. In only three years' time this movement had over 3,500 offices and attracted over 100,000 to meetings in 75 cities across the nation. Thus, businessmen led the way in accepting the challenge of the young, and it was these businessmen and their wives, in thousands of women's missionary societies or women's Penny Bands, which provided the much-needed money to send the youth who were on fire to go.

Ralph and I and the young people who shared our dream had often talked of that time. Could God do it again? One of the young men in our group, only a junior at Caltech, had said, "Yes, He can, and He will. We need to tell the students He is still counting on them," and almost single-handedly Bill Haines started the first of a series of Student Conferences on World Evangelization. At the time we wondered who would pay the $2400 bill for the two-day rental of one of the most prestigious auditoriums in Pasadena — the Beckman Auditorium on the campus of Caltech. Ralph and I couldn't believe that in five months, a fulltime student could arouse enough interest among Christian students to fill that building. But 650 had come.

"The students have the vision. They have the stamina and the will. If we only could find adults with the same drive," sighed Ralph. Remembering those eager people 75 years ago, Ralph asked our staff that brainstorming day, "How will *we* go about arousing the interest of evangelical Christians? We can't do it alone, and we don't have to. But what can we do that nobody else is doing to make Christians see that the day of pioneer, frontier missions is not over?"

And the ideas began to come.

"We need to push those SCOWE conferences more. No one is really organizing them methodically. Someone needs to." one said.

"How about assigning someone to write Sunday School materials on the present needs? This will require a lot of research on hidden people groups. We'll have to get acquainted with their children well enough to write interesting stories for children. But we've got to start with the children as well as with adults. They know far more about TV personalities than they should; if we could just open up their world and win them to Christ's cause at the same time. We really must!"

"But the adults," someone else said, "how can we arouse their interest? They love the Lord; they swarm to Bible study groups, but they stay away in droves from missionary meetings. How can we turn them around?"

"We've got to set up prayer groups," another suggested.

"That's true, but how will we get them to come?"

"You know, when I was at UCLA, I was the only Christian student in our dorm of 90 who was the least bit interested in missions. I guess I really bugged the group about missions because one day the student leader told me he was praying for me that I would get off this kick and get back to what God was interested in — discipleship and evangelism here!" Beth laughed, and went on, "I challenged him to read just four books and to let me have ten minutes of each of our housemeeting times to give a capsule report on some unreached people — you know, where they were on the map, what the newspapers were saying about them, etc. Even I couldn't have guessed that in a few months' time ten of those students would be so gung-ho for missions that others would be praying for them too to 'get off that missions kick,' " and she laughed again. "What I'm saying, I guess, is that somehow we have to get the people — the churches — more personally acquainted with those who need reaching."

"And maps, and newspaper articles, and research is a way to start?"

"Yes, and why can't we do a National Geographic-type Unreached Peoples magazine with good pictures and articles, and take subscriptions for it? Or send a roving photographer around the world to take movies, or video tapes?" Ralph suggested.

"Boy," I thought, "are we getting wild! But wouldn't it be great if we could? Wouldn't it be just great! Maybe, in God's providence and time . . ."

42

NOVEMBER 1977 - JANUARY 1978 "ALL THINGS SHALL BE ADDED" (Matthew 6:33)

October 1st and then Oct. 7th had come and gone. Through a series of miracles God had provided just barely enough money for us to enter into escrow. We were past that first great crisis.

At first glance, nothing had changed. We occupied the same amount of space: we couldn't afford to spread out, even though with God's grace we might in a year technically own the entire campus. The cult still occupied most of the campus since their two-year lease would not expire for almost another year, July 31st, 1978.

Nothing seemed changed — except the volume of mail! Where we had been getting a huge stack of letters and thousands of dollars every day, now there was only a trickle. We still had millions of dollars left to pay and actually owed $300,000. Now that the crisis was past the well was dry.

There were other changes too. Summer staff returned to their regular jobs or to school, and we were back to a near-skeleton crew. Those who felt the Lord leading them to apply for permanent staff assignments came empty handed, literally. They had worked all summer for nothing, paying their own room and board. Now their bank and savings accounts were depleted, yet they had to eat. We knew that many mission boards accepted candidates only *after* they had raised their support. But if we had followed that policy we would never have started; we couldn't have! Would churches and friends give on a monthly basis to support these staff members? We knew they did when these people were joining long-established missions. How about when they were joining our staff? Such a new, relatively unknown project? Certainly raising support had to be a high priority.

Again we thanked the Lord for Prudence and her years of experience with Campus Crusade. She taught our staff all we know about writing support letters, explaining our work to all sorts of friends, setting up special times to tell about the Center and its goals. "It usually takes two to six months to raise your support," she told us. "We'd like to give all our staff members that much time, but we can't. There is no one to replace us while we would be away. We'll give each one at least a half day a month, though, to work on support letters and accounts. One at a time we'll take off for more intensive support raising."

And we busily began writing letters and talking to friends and church mission committees about our personal needs. Had it only been one year since Ralph and I had gone through that same desperate letter writing? I remembered the time we sent special delivery letters to pastors, old friends of ours — special delivery because the mission budgets of their churches were at those very moments being decided. And I remembered the elation and dismay we felt as some letters came back with sure promises of support and others with comments of "Sorry, you're too late." Some never answered at all. How I wished God would supply without all that frantic correspondence. I knew He could, but He didn't. But having to raise our own support we came to find God's blessing in disguise.

Almost daily we would receive letters from someone out of a job who would like to work at the Center. Prudence sorted these people out, carefully. Were they spiritually qualified? Were their hearts in missions? Or were they just looking for a job? Prudence always told applicants, "We have a policy here like most mission boards have today, and this is, you will have to raise your own support. Even if we could offer you a salary, someone would have to raise that money. Often the person being supported is the best one to do that since his friends are more likely to give to him than to an organization as such. We will help you as much as we can, give you guidelines and supervise your efforts. But we believe that if the Lord wants you here, He will verify this by helping you get your support. **Everyone on staff is doing the same. Can you** accept this policy?"

With dismay we saw some people we thought extremely desirable say, "Oh," and drift away. But we learned a valuable lesson.

I had been reading about Gideon again. He was called from the farm to lead an army. He had no leadership experience whatsoever, nor was there any logical reason why anyone would follow him. Yet 32,000 men gathered to fight with him. How he must have praised God for those men! But God said, " 'There are too many of you! I can't let all of you fight the Midianites, for then the people of Israel will boast to me that they saved themselves by their own strength! Send home any of your men who are timid and frightened!' So first twenty-two thousand of them left, yet the Lord told Gideon, 'There are still too many.'"

How on earth do Gideon and finding staff go together? Unless one can believe that God will supply his personal daily financial needs, there is no way he can believe that God will supply a million dollars out of nowhere. In other words, although we had not realized it (nor would have planned it that way), our total inability to pay salaries was God's provision to test the faith of our applicants. Would they be able to stand with us when the going became rough? We also knew that no one could say we succeeded because we were so wise, so skilled in fund raising, so professional, so many, or so talented. The staff we have are bright, eager, and talented, mainly young people. Their training lies in the fields of engineering, science, nursing, teaching, and pastoral work, rather than in fund raising, graphic arts, or administration. Yet God has used them. We have produced no miracles. We don't know how. And we don't have the money to hire miracle workers. Like Gideon, we must rely on God.

43

APRIL 1978
TEMPTATION COMES

January came, then February and March. According to our original schedule we should have been completing our down payment of 1.5 million on April 1st. It was very fortunate the college owners had extended that deadline to September 1, 1978 — because April 1st we had nothing, absolutely nothing! We had received one sizable gift which had paid off one of our loans. But we still owed $175,000 on last October's loans and needed another $650,000 come September plus $280,000 for the off-campus housing on October 1st, 1978. All those intervening weeks we had worked madly, planning World Awareness Seminars to be presented in churches, writing brochures, running our first Institute of International Studies for college students (in January), working out an historical chart of the expansion of the gospel for use in churches, and as always continuing to raise personal support. Ralph had been to Brazil, the Philippines, Hong Kong, Atlanta, and Montreat, North Carolina where he had spoken at missions conferences, acted as a consultant or helped set up overseas Centers for Frontier Missions, of which there were now four.

But what about the money? Ralph was convinced that God did not want us to raid current mission budgets nor do an expensive mass mailing campaign in order to raise the money we needed.

We knew that the $850,000 we had already put down was only part of the down payment, and we could still lose the campus to the cult on our doorstep. One of our staff, on a day off, out of curiosity had visited their newly acquired property in a hilly area near the ocean and he reported that although it was a beautiful site, there were only two large buildings and two sheds on the property. *Moreover, there was no sign of any new construction about to begin.* Thus we knew that Summit still wanted this campus and hoped and chanted prayers that we default on completing our payment, thereby pulling out of escrow and leaving the property to the highest bidder. We could hear the chants, often late at night and very early in the morning. And compared to the number of cult followers on the main campus, we felt so few and alone.

But we were not alone. One by one more staff came to join us. Some were young, eager to see the world reached for Christ NOW! Others were more mature people who had battled Satan for many long years.

Dr. Norman Lewis, the widely known author of books on faith-promise giving, had left his church in Portland the previous December and now served as a much-needed associate director, taking Hal Leaman's place. He spoke about the Center here and there, checked and double-checked brochures in the making, and generally helped direct traffic. Dr. Ben Jennings left his church in April and became our contact with churches all over the country. In May Dr. George Peters from Dallas Seminary accepted the position of International Director, ready in his many already-scheduled travels to help establish and maintain contact with the overseas sister centers. Don Richardson of Regions Beyond Missionary Union and author of *Peace Child* found a house where he could move his family when they came in July. Paul Herman, at one time the U.S. competitor for the decathlon at the Olympics and a man whose heart had long been in tribal work, preceded Don on campus, starting plans for the Tribal Studies Center and also helping in general staff recruitment.

Our Million Person Campaign was also now underway. We were convinced that even though we needed more than a million dollars by September 1st, we needed even more to awaken at least a million U.S. evangelicals to the crisis in missions. We were really tempted to try for the big money. "After all, it belongs to God, and this certainly is His cause," we told ourselves.

Yet always we felt checked. God could bring huge gifts to us, if He chose, but we were to use the rod in our hand (like Moses), or the slingshot (like David), the pitchers and lamps (like Gideon), or the five loaves and two fish (like Andrew). We felt somehow that God wanted to do a great thing with the $15 gifts common, ordinary (even poor) people could give.

But how could the few on our staff suddenly reach out to touch and change the perspective of a million people?

For months Bob and Darwin had been working on a slide show which depicted the advance of Christianity and the fields yet unharvested. These World Awareness Seminars were designed for use in churches or in private living rooms. Bob and Darwin had worked out a two page mini-course which hopefully would pique the interest of all who read it to investigate further into the need for missions. We carefully designed and then printed 100,000 individually numbered decision cards to register as "World Christians" all who read the mini-course and promised to pray and study further about the unreached peoples of the world. Each registrant was also asked to give $15 to help secure the campus as a center from which could flow information and inspiration about these people.

We were busy as could be. So was Satan. Tickets for plane flights were unaccountably misplaced (and found just in time!); cars would break down, once just as we arrived at the airport. Staff took turns in bed with the flu. And as always we had our detractors who constantly assured us (and others) that we would never succeed.

In April Summit asked for permission to rent from us when (and if?) we got the campus in August, promising to pay $30,000 a month for rent. Thirty thousand a month!

"If you will fall down and worship me, I'll give you the kingdoms of the earth," our ancient Enemy had told Jesus. That same enemy knew we needed that money, and tempted us also.

"No! We can't get the money we need that way. In the Old Testament many of the kings destroyed all sorts of evil, but still allowed the 'high places' for idol worship to remain, and God was displeased. To allow the Buddha to stay on campus, now with our permission, and to allow worship we know is displeasing to God would be wrong. When we had no authority over the situation that was different. But on September 1st we will become legal owners. No, we can't do it!" we all felt.

"That means of course that we will have to fill the campus some other way by fall," Ralph reminded us.

So we went to our knees again.

44

MAY 1978
"MY WAYS ARE HIGHER
THAN YOUR WAYS"
(Isaiah 55:8)

For some years Ralph had been concerned about the need to challenge students in America to go to the unreached places, to the 2.4 billion that nobody was even trying to reach with the gospel. After the Inter-Varsity Urbana meeting of December, 1973, he had started the Summer Institute of International Studies, and by now 350 students had been "turned on" to the cause of missions by what they had learned there. But only 350 students over a four-year period was such a trickle!

"Somehow we've got to get to larger numbers of young people," Ralph kept insisting.

Some of the SIIS board members had become a bit irritated at this. "We're doing a quality job. If we get too many students, we won't have the sense of community we now have with them. Something will be lost," they replied.

And being only one voice among several. Ralph acquiesced. But he dreamed of working more effectively toward a true *movement* for missions.

Now in late April of 1978 God seemed to speak to him. "That's the answer. You see the need for students to catch fire. You know what that will mean to the 'unwon' peoples of the world. And you know what that will do to the churches at home. Here's your chance. You need to fill this campus. And you want thousands of students to open their eyes and truly see the fields still needing to be harvested. Can't you see that the two fit together?"

And Ralph set his jaw and came back to a much-overworked staff.

"I have a feeling God is giving us a kick in the pants. We've always intended, down the road a bit, to fill this campus with college students, students coming for only one concentrated semester of mission studies. We'll have to accelerate our plans. We need at least 700 by fall," Ralph announced.

We all gasped. Seven hundred students! Where would we get them? How could we be ready for them in time? Who would do the recruitment and the planning? If we got the students, what about beds, linens, pots and pans? The idea was overwhelming.

And who on our small staff could be shifted to the new task?

But when Ralph spelled out the alternatives, we agreed it was the only way.

Clearly, if we allowed Summit to stay, half our constituency would be totally outraged — they had given us funds to end their presence on the campus and in the community, where they had even infiltrated local Boy and Girl Scout Troops. On the other hand, there were business people who had a different perspective. You could hear some of them who had given generously saying, "You are promoting young people to go to India to live totally surrounded by Hindus; why can't you, for $30,000 a month, allow "American Hindus" to live across the street? You'll throw away more money in one month than we can give in a year!"

Clearly we had to do our best to *fill* the campus, not just *fund* it.

It was as though we had come full circle. In explaining our mission to people, we had all along stressed as our highest priority the tracking down of the hidden people of the world. We knew these numbered more than half the world's population. We wanted it to be impossible for Christians to sit at ease, content to do things of secondary importance while the tremendous need went untouched. Thus for some time we had told people that our first priority was the hidden people. And, second, we had placed the task of arousing evangelicals to become aware of the need and to do something about it. Only in third place had we placed the desire to train college students for one special semester so that they would have an entirely new, worldwide perspective.

All of a sudden all this was changed, through no choice of our own. Now, unavoidably, we had to have 700 students by fall. Now, unavoidably, we had to change the perspective of a million evangelicals or we would lose this campus completely to a Hindu cult trying with all its might to win the souls of American "Christians". But what about our first priority? What about those hidden 2.4 billion people who still needed the gospel? Did the Lord have reasons for interposing these other tasks?

We struggled with those questions, and like Mary we thought long thoughts about how God's ways are not like our ways. Perhaps these intermediate tasks were His way of accomplishing the highest priority. Perhaps we were just not wise enough to see that certain foundations had to be laid before the highest priority could be confronted effectively.

"O.K., God," we said. "If that's the way You want it, that's fine." And we realized that, yes, this *was* the proper time to go all out for college students. Not only was this period in their lives crucial, but it was a crucial first in the order of implementing the vision of the Center. With a flood of students would come a flood of young faith, bustle, visibility, ties to home churches and to colleges to which they would return. These students would help reach the million people much faster, and the million people's new World Christian decisions and $15 one-time gifts to the Center would come sooner too. Yes, God did know best!

But could we do it all soon enough? Could we get the money we must have by September if we also spent a lot of time attracting those students and preparing for them? Our hearts quailed, but the Lord pointed out to us other promises:

"Search the Book of the Lord and see all that He will do; not one detail will He miss . . . for the Lord has said it, and His Spirit will make it all come true" (Isa. 34:16), and "Not by might, nor by power, but by my Spirit, says the Lord of Hosts — you will succeed because of my Spirit, though you are few and weak . . . Do not despise this small beginning, for the eyes of the Lord rejoice to see the work begin . . ." (Zech. 4:6b, 10a)

What a beginning!

45

MAY 1978
"BEFORE YOU CALL
I WILL ANSWER"
(Isaiah 65:24)

"Ralph, we're really concerned about you people down there. Several of us are coming down to see you on Thursday."

It was Gene Davis on the phone again. They knew the money just wasn't coming in. They had given too much to give up now. And they truly believed, as we did, that God wanted this campus for missions.

That was in March. We on staff were delighted to see them come because these were men that were with us *one hundred per cent*. But we were discouraged when they left. They had great plans for what they would do for us to help raise the money, but everything they suggested was long range — it would bring in money after

September. One idea was another film like we had made the summer before, but better this time.

"When can it be done?" we asked.

"Toward the end of summer," they answered.

"Oh," we said. And nothing more. But our thoughts were, "Well, we obviously can't count on them for help now. They mean well, but it just isn't good enough."

Somewhere in the next two months that scheduling changed drastically. Dale Kietzman wrote a script. Ray Carlson of International Films on our campus started taking movie footage, and before we knew it a film was in the making.

Those Oregon businessmen — Gene Davis, Dave Adams, and now two or three others — organized their own modern-day Laymen's Missionary Movement — The World Christian Associates — with their first project being the Center. They agreed to fund this movie and to stick with us until we reached our goal. They visited us frequently and prayed constantly on our behalf.

Ray, busy at work on the film, felt we needed some well-known person to narrate it. Who could it be? And his mind went back immediately to the previous fall.

"Do you think Pat Boone will help us once more?" he asked Ralph. "Because of his previous involvement he would be the best one we could get to narrate the film."

It takes a certain amount of nerve to ask a person like Pat Boone for a favor like that, especially for a second time. His daughter Debbie had just won an Oscar for her song "You Light Up My Life" and we saw by the newspapers that she and her father were performing together in Las Vegas. Every few days Ray Carlson called Ralph and asked, "Have you called Pat Boone's office yet?" And every day Ralph would give some excuse or other — he hadn't had time; he had visitors in his office all day; he knew Pat wasn't in town ... Finally one day he did call. As before, Jan, Pat's secretary, was warmly cordial. She wanted to know how things were going, what the Lord was doing for us now, how they could help.

And Ralph told her what we needed.

"Pat will be in Las Vegas until next Wednesday. He'll come home for only ten days and then he'll be gone for another six weeks." She sounded a bit hesitant. "But I'll talk to him," she added.

Not everyone on Pat's staff shared her attitude. After all, hadn't Pat done enough for us already? We understood their reluctance, yet felt somehow that perhaps God would do this one more miracle for us.

"Ralph, why don't you write Pat a letter and explain why we need him," Ray insisted. It just might make the difference.

It was a couple of days before Ralph could get to the letter. And as he was well into writing it, the phone rang. It was Ray calling.

"Ralph, Pat's office just called. Pat says he'll be glad to help us. Praise the Lord!"

When Ralph reported all this to the staff, the verse crossed my mind, "I will answer them before they even call to me. While they are still talking to me about their needs, I will go ahead and answer their prayers!" (Isa. 65:24LB) Our hearts breathed, "Thank you, Lord. How very faithful you are!"

46

MAY 15, 1978
MORE BATTLES AND
MORE TROOPS

Ralph sat listening, the phone to his ear. I could tell something serious was being discussed — something serious and a bit painful. Charlie Mellis, the director for the last three years of the Summer Institute of International Studies, had called to say that because of low enrollment the program would have to be cancelled.

For several weeks we had heard that the SIIS was in trouble, and our younger staff, almost all SIIS alumni, were very concerned. "They just can't cancel it! To start it up again will be twice as hard. Anyhow, the young people of this country need that program," they insisted. But there it was. To break even financially at the University of Colorado campus in Boulder there had to be at least sixty students, and only thirty had registered.

"Hey, Dad, why can't we have it here?" our son-in-law suggested. "We had only thirty students for our winter course and came out O.K. Anyhow, many of the professors come from this area, and we won't have their travel to pay. That will be a savings."

"You realize, Brad, that with Bruce and Christy in India lining up the overseas follow-up for our winter course, we have no one to direct this one. Charlie says he doesn't feel that he can. That means someone from our staff would have to do it. Do you think Beth can handle the personnel office by herself?"

There were several adjustments that had to be made, and some negotiations with Charlie, but by mid-May, we had been put in charge of the SIIS program for that summer.

Just about that time, Dr. Clyde Taylor in Washington, D.C. called Ralph about a possible staff member, a man very skilled in management who was just retiring as a Commander from the U.S. Navy. Lee Holthaus came out for a few days and impressed us all. "He's just what we need. But will he come?"

Dr. Taylor himself came two weeks later, and from the first moment was deep in work, advising here, suggesting there. Our staff fell in love with this grand old missions statesman. "Unfortunately," he said, "I can't move out here to help you permanently, but I am willing to do what I can there. Also, Lee and his family have decided to come and join your staff. That should help."

We were assembling our troops for the last march. Summer had come; our crisis date was three months away — only twelve short weeks. Now God was sending us not only the foot soldiers we needed. He was also sending commanders.

We were ready to march.

47

JUNE 1978
WHAT DO YOU HOLD
IN YOUR HAND?

"What do you hold in your hand today?
To whom or to what are you bound?
Are you willing to give it to God right now?
Give it up, let it go, throw it down!"

Through blinded eyes I searched frantically in
my purse for a handerchief and ended up em-
barrassedly catching the tears with the back of
my hand. High up front on the platform, Pat
Taylor was singing "Moses", a sermon in song
written by the blind composer, Ken Medema.

It was June, 1978 a little less than two years
from the time we had embarked alone on this
great adventure. As I listened, I relived with
Moses that helpless sense of loneliness in a job

that was just too great. And with Moses, I again dedicated the little we had in our hands to His use, for His purposes, for Him to somehow multiply to fit that awesome need.

For a long time I had been trying to write the story of the U.S. Center for World Mission. I had felt totally inadequate for even that job, having never written anything before other than one published article. Yet because there was no one else to do it, no one else who had been with us from the very beginning of the project, it had to be my job. So I had turned my "rod" — my pen — over to Him, asking that somehow I would be able to tell the wonders He had done in our midst and thereby, hopefully, bring glory to His name. In writing I had again walked in memory around the campus, climbed the heights of victory and wept in the valleys of despair which we had experienced. Now the book was almost done, but the memories were still fresh. That was why, listening to Pat sing, I felt related to Moses in a new, painful yet joyous way. We too had stood on holy ground. We too had heard the "voice" speaking to us. We too had turned over our own inadequacies and had seen God use them to work His miracles.

It is now exactly a year since I sat there. And it is almost a year since that book went to press for the first time. This past year will also have its book, still being written. But here let me only say that that year too has had its miracles — of desperately needed money coming in right on time, of staff appearing out of nowhere, of graciousness on the part of the College authorities, and of many, many people who have helped us at difficult junctures. This year has also been a year of severe testing for us all. Sometimes we could not make our payments. Sometimes the faith of many of our staff quavered and almost, it seemed, disappeared. We have suffered severe criticism within and without. But through it all we have known the joy and comfort of God's presence in the midst of the furnace. Through it all we have seen our wonderful younger staff changed into mature Christian leaders. What last year would have caused them to express frustration and perhaps even bitterness, they now take with patience and grace. It's as if in asking for "gold" to meet our payments, still heavy upon us every three months, God is manufacturing "gold" in the personalities of our staff. And we stand back amazed and awed by His more perfect answer to our prayers.

Part of the problem lay in Ralph's conviction that God wanted us not to ask any individual for more than $15.95. If God wanted people to give more, He would have to lay it on their hearts. We could approach foundations, where it seemed reasonable. We could ask churches to help us — but only over and beyond whatever they were already doing in missions. To accomplish what God had told us to do, we did not feel free to perhaps destroy what He had told others to do.

So long as the money was coming in steadily, just before our September 1978 deadline, this approach didn't cause much concern to our staff and close friends. But when quarterly payments came due and had to be renegotiated or postponed, a storm arose. Ralph was accused by some of stubbornly trying to destroy what God had already done. It was hard not to believe this when told that professional fundraisers working for other Christian organizations had publicly ridiculed our fund raising approach as the classic example of how *not* to do it. Friends argued that since we were doing God's will, we should not worry about hurting the support base of other agencies, that we were being ridiculously circumspect. Ralph's leadership was challenged, his motives questioned. How easy it would have been to follow this advice. How easy to indiscriminately raid church budgets, woo away regular supporters from other agencies, take a "me first" attitude through it all. And with so much criticism from so many sources, it was a temptation.

We knew that not everyone who "Attempted great things for God" was successful. Our historical studies had warned us that many things obviously in God's will had failed to come to fruition. The whole cause of Protestant missions was delayed 200 years because those who should have backed Justinian Welz, didn't. In another case, because of a wrong decision by well-meaning non-missionaries in places of authority, an open door to China slammed shut and remained so for another 200 years. Yet we also knew that not everyone who believes he is led of God is so led. How often I yearned for the sure voice that Moses heard, the voice no one could doubt.

And yet, deep within our own hearts, we heard that voice. We didn't, indeed dared not, rely on what *others* felt or cared *must* be His will. Then we understood the cross behind William Carey's magnificent challenge, "Attempt great things for God; expect great things from God."

Our confirmation of God's voice came in the assurances of mission agency after mission agency that they were behind us. Sometimes it was the letters from their missionaries, including their own much-needed $15.95 check. Just as often it was the top mission executives sending us a $15.95 gift for every member of their Board of Directors. Or simply assuring us of their prayers and offering to send out our brochures, and encouraging their young prospective candidates to get into our Institute of International Studies program. Or expressing appreciation that our approach would not harm, but help them. Pastors, on the other hand, not used to one-time appeals, sometimes feared sharing our challenge with their members lest their own building program suffer. So they would send, say, $5,000.00 from the Mission Budget, not understanding that there is a big difference between $5,000.00 from a budget about which the congregation knows little and $5,000.00 coming from 313 now-awakened members of their congregation. But sitting where we did, we saw the churches where the vision was shared coming alive, caught up in the sense that "God is doing a mighty work in our time — and he is using us in it." One pastor elatedly recorded that as a result of hearing our challenge that in his congregation, their regular giving to missions had tripled in one year. How we rejoiced at that!

Within five years we hope to complete the founding of the Center. But by then we also hope to have broadened the mission awareness of 200,000 young people, and to have awakened a million evangelicals to the remaining harvest to such an extent that they will be ready to send these young people — at least 35,000 of them overseas. Many will also go from Africa and from Asia; but we know, as does every mission leader, that many will still have to go from America.

The process of growth has been slow, but steady. "The only problem," Ralph told me once, "is that it's in the early stages when our payments are largest that the growth is slower. A lot of people have to have a chance to hear about us, and that takes time. But they will, if people keep passing the vision to others."

That was one thing we did not at first understand about the small, one-time gift process. The appeal is so mild that people can cheerfully pass it on, share it with others, without transgressing that invisible barrier of American culture that normally forbids our meddling in other people's affairs. Without any pressure from us, many were passing on the vision. We have heard incredible stories about someone indeed just happening to get a book from a passing tourist, or a farmer in Winnipeg whose wife was handed a book, or someone who saw one on a rack in the grocery store, read it and passed it on. Most of the time those who read the book sent in a gift.

At the precise time when the growth was most steady, though still small, and when we were in better shape financially than we had ever been, people started saying, "What will you do if you can't make it?" or, "Why don't you forget about the whole campus? Just buy one building," or "Why don't you just give up and go elsewhere?"

But we knew that never again would we be able to buy this kind of campus at this kind of price. Close to a major airport of the world, close to 17 major universities with their research libraries. Never again would we be able to buy a whole campus for what one major new building might cost. All of this in the middle of the world's most diverse collection of peoples — southern California is virtually a Pentecost of Nations.

"Then if you must stay with this, at least be sensible and get the money wherever you can. God helps those who help themselves. Come on, now, you'll never make it with this $15.00 plan. Never in the world," we were told again and again and again.

For months Ralph and I prayed about the matter. But we could not shake the conviction that the small, one-time gift approach was God's way for us. He could also provide large gifts, if He wished. This we have abundantly found out. And we have accepted these also as from His gracious, loving hand.

We knew that the crux of the problem lay not in the $15.95 amount so much as in the difficulty of finding a million evangelicals to vote with their money just once for this cause. In the 2½ years since we began, 11,000 have done so. But by September 1979 we would need to have 44,000 more such gifts. More people would have to not only grasp the vision themselves but also pass it on to others. How could we encourage them to do so?

Like Moses, again, we started with what was in our hands. We had a Jericho book, a circle chart, a movie, and a grapevine letter. We had the goodwill of Christian leaders and mission executives from all over the country. And we had 11,000 people praying for us, many asking "How can I help?" Most, like us, had little money. But perhaps all had something that God could use.

Take Ralph's father, for instance. Eighty-three years old and long a Godly Christian, he had been faithful in his prayers and support of the Center. Our first year on campus he walked with us in summer's heat those seven long Jericho marches. I often wondered if he would have a heart attack and die while marching. Yet he insisted on participating, all seven Sunday afternoons.

It's barely two years since then, and Daddy is becoming a bit frail. It is not now quite as easy for him to get in and out of our car when he comes to help out on Thursdays. He can't go on camping trips anymore. But he has wanted to help.

Moses had a rod which God used. Daddy has had a book — the first edition of this one. He also has had a built-in audience, you might say: he lives in a retirement home.

We didn't think much about it when he asked for a second copy of the book and brought in a check from someone who had read his. But when he asked for two more and each week brought in more and more checks, we asked him about it.

"Why don't we just give you a number of books to pass out?" Ralph asked him.

"Oh, no! I just want a few. I just keep lending them out to different people. That way they know someone else is waiting to read them, and thus don't just put them aside to read later. "And," he chuckled, "if they don't get them back to me fairly soon, I can ask when they'll be through. That way I'm sure they are reading them."

We wouldn't have imagined a man that age could have been one of our most effective multipliers. Fifty people have now read his books, and well over half have given a gift of $15.95.

Another example involved the help of three widely separated people. Dr. Donald McGavran, perhaps the foremost missionary strategist in the world today, and a dear friend of ours, at his own expense sent out a letter to all the missionary subscribers to the *Church Growth Bulletin*. In it he requested them to ask each of their supporters to send us a one-time $15.00 gift. One of these missionaries did precisely that. The lady who regularly sent out her prayer letters for her was startled and intrigued, but also a bit put upon, when asked to send out an extra letter for her missionary friend. But since she lived just a few miles away and yet had never heard of us, she came over to investigate. And she wasn't one bit impressed — at first. Our receptionist — our youngest daughter — was alone in the front lobby. Our building was very unpretentious, being furnished with donated or government surplus office furniture. There were no plush carpets, nor soft lounge chairs.

But she started to talk with Tricia. Tricia showed her our literature, explained to her our purposes, told her our dreams, and asked for her prayers. I crossed the lobby just as this lady was turning to leave and saw Tricia thrust my book into her hands, saying, "Oh, before you read this other literature, read this book. It explains better than anything." And I wondered idly if Tricia, at eighteen, was mature enough and long enough on the job to be trusted to explain by herself all that was necessary. But our deadline was just weeks away, and everyone was simply overloaded with too much work. Tricia had to be sufficient.

The next morning in the middle of our staff prayer time Tricia was called to the phone. She returned beaming. "That was Mary . . ." she said, "you know, the lady that was asking all those questions yesterday. Well, guess what! She's already called the headquarters of World Evangelization Crusade. They told her she could send a letter to more than just this one missionary's supporters. They're sending her a large list today. And hear this, she personally will pay the postage if we will do the mailing. She's on her way right now with a draft of her letter and a $500 check.

Dr. McGavran's letter brought in other responses as well. But perhaps more than anything else, it helped us to put together what we came to call our grapevine letter. By this means we hoped to use the grapevine to reach that million people. Each person contributing was asked to send the letter to three of his or her friends, explaining (with materials we provide) the vision, the need, and our current crisis. The letter asks them to give $15.95 and also send three grapevine letters themselves to three of their friends. What system could be more elementary? And yet in God's grace, it could work. And it has, not always in great volume, but steadily and growing.

Some churches as denominations have sent out that letter, asking each of their members to each send out three copies of it. Three mission agencies (MAF, OC, and WO) are sending out special letters asking their supporters to reach other Christians on our behalf.

Some would-be helpers have come up with even more novel ideas. Two ladies from a large church in Denver heard about us, came for a few days to check us out, and went home, excited and praying about how they could help. They're launching the idea of "dining with a purpose" — a series of chain dinners, as it were, where guests at the first invite still others to their own homes, who do the same again. At each dinner, the vision and need of the Center is presented and the guests challenged to help with their own $15.95 gifts and in turn to host a similar dinner.

One man sent us a $15.95 check for himself and then decided to multiply it be sending in the same amount in advance for twenty of his friends. He notified each of what he had done, and then asked them to do the same with twenty of their friends. Again a grapevine concept, with a new twist.

Another suggested our name to a foundation, one completely unknown to us, which sent us a gift, right at a very critical time. Another borrowed our "Penetrating the Last Frontiers" film and showed it in 15 different churches.

A local pastor asked for 4,000 copies of this second edition of the Jericho book to give to his congregation on his birthday.

"What do you hold in your hand today?" Again the words swept over me as I looked back on the year since I had first heard them. Moses' rod was a simple shepherd's stick, but God used it to do all sorts of miracles. Would simple things in the hands of ordinary people who loved God be sufficient to meet our last really large quarterly payment of $660,000 on Sept. 15th? And what about the (smaller) quarterly payments after that? We had bought a campus for ⅓ the replacement cost. Had we been foolish? Had we perhaps misunderstood God's guidance? Were we putting Him to the test in a way that was wrong?

Or had He put us in this place to show Himself strong in our behalf?

Epilogue

JULY 1979
"FORWARD MARCH"
(Exodus 14:15)

It is now the first week in July. We are "over the Jordan." For nine months we have occupied the entire campus, going through building after building and cleansing them from all Satanic forces, rededicating them to the Lord of lords, the God who is above all gods, the Master of the harvest.

In a real sense the battle for the promised land is still on. So long as Joshua was on the far side of the Jordan, he could retreat. But once across, there was no way to go but forward.

That's where we are. We can still lose the campus. We owe $660,000 in September. But like Joshua, now there is no retreat. If we fail to make that payment, we lose the campus and the $1.5 million we have already put down as well. The Jordan river is behind us; the walls of Jericho are down but other walled cities remain.

Is the God who parted the river able also to make those walls tumble?

So the battle for the new land goes on. It is as though this year, too, we have marched around other cities once, twice, three times, believing and praying every step of the way. Like Moses when God called him to an impossible task, we sometimes feel, "Who are we that we should do this? We can't talk well. We don't know how to raise funds. We're not famous nor rich." And like then, God answers us, "Who makes mouths? Isn't it I, the Lord? Who makes a man so that he can speak or not speak, see or not see, hear or not hear? Now go ahead and do as I tell you, for I will help you. . ." (Exodus 4:11-12a).

And we remember, shamefaced, that He also said "The silver and gold are mine. All the people of the earth are mine. There is nothing too hard for me."

We think of the cult, trying so very hard to win men to an empty mixture of the major religions of the world, looking inward for the God-self to find answers. We see the tremendous task around the world. How can we Christians ever reach the now 2.5 billion, increasing every day that we neglect them? What an impossible job Jesus left for those few who gathered in the upper room that day in Jerusalem! But then there were only twelve plus a few others. Now one-third of the world's population at least *claims* to be Christian.

But he didn't expect them to do it alone. Neither does He expect us to do it alone. He has sent the Holy Spirit to be with us, to be the "Commander-in-Chief" of the Lord's army (See Joshua 5:14).

And He has told us, "I am God; there is no other; I have sworn by myself and I will never go back on my word, for it is true — that every knee in all the world *shall* bow to me, and every tongue *shall* swear allegiance to my name" (Isa. 45:22-23). Victory is surely His, just as surely as the sun rises and sets every day.

So we continue to march and to trust and pray.

How do you finish a story that isn't finished? You just keep marching, in faith. . .

ONCE MORE AROUND JERICHO

What is this
all about?

THE HIDDEN PEOPLES:
the last frontiers

In 1961 a small metallic object rocketed into airless space and began to circle the earth. Overnight, a startled world stepped hesitantly into the space age. Within ten years the same world watched as a man named Armstrong stepped down on the moon. As a result, modern man plunged into an awareness of a new frontier.

THE FIRST ERA--1792

A similar new awareness startled English-speaking Christians almost two hundred years earlier when a man named William Carey wrote a small book that confronted his readers with a massive omission. His basic facts and figures proved their obligation to reach the heathen nations with the Gospel. As a result, after almost three centuries of virtually no Protestant outreach, a dozen mission societies sprang into existence, and what was to become a flood tide of evangelical mission activities began to reach every corner of the globe. This was the first stage of Protestant missions.

THE SECOND ERA--1865

However, almost as soon as mission work
began to succeed in Africa and Asia, missionaries came to be overwhelmingly preoccupied
with the growing national churches they
established, and became less and less aware
of peoples still unreached--a second massive
omission. Eventually, in 1865, Hudson Taylor
launched the second stage of Protestant missions
by shifting the gaze of mission leaders from the
coastlands to the inland areas. He crossed this
geographical frontier and jolted the Christians
of his day not only with a new awareness of
vast areas of hidden people but with a new
means to reach them, and the massive new
"faith mission" movement was born.

This new thrust sparked recurrent attention
to new frontiers throughout the next 100 years
of unprecedented Christian growth until toady
almost half the people in the world are either
committed to Christ or at least claim to be
Christians.

But the unbelievable impact of Christian
missions upon the world can hardly be measured
in its full scope. It has spanned oceans and
coastlands and reached inland frontiers and, in
those particular cultures which it has penetrated,
it has become a transforming power. Quite
understandably, it has also typically become
overwhelmingly preoccupied with the mushroom-
ing obligations of its success. Revivals are like
a fire out of control in many parts of Africa,
Latin America, Indonesia and Korea, with 1,000
new churches opening their doors each week.
Just to keep up with the needs of this growing
movement consumes virtually all present mission
efforts.

THE THIRD ERA--Today!

Thus it is a quite disturbing new awareness
in the midst of this success to discover that all
those thousands of language and cultural pockets
now penetrated contain one out of five of the
world's non-Christians. The bombshell confrontation for our time is not quite the same as

Carey's (the "heathens" can and must be reached)
or Taylor's (we've forgotten the inland peoples)
but rather, *what about the 4 out of 5 non-Christians who are still beyond invisible cultural frontiers?*

Careful studies first presented at the International Congress on World Evangelization at
Lausanne, Switzerland, introduced the concept
of the remaining *cultural* frontiers to be spanned
in order for 80% of the world's non-Christians to
be won to Christ.

More precisely, of 3,060 million non-Christians
in the world today, 2,456 million are beyond
these invisible, cultural frontiers. Nearly a
billion Chinese with about half a billion each of
Muslims, Hindus, and other tribal or Asian people,
are locked within a mosaic of subcultures, language
barriers and social prejudices where as yet no
viable Christian church has been founded. Yet,
these are the problems which faced the Apostle
Paul and 2000 years of missionary outreach.
Would you like to visualize how many people that
is? Preaching to 60,000 different people per
day in this group would take you over 100 years
to touch 2,456 million people!

The tragedy is not in the obstacles. This is
nothing new in the story of the spread of the
Gospel. The tragedy is that less than 1% of all
Christian workers are concentrating on these 2.5
billion lost and furthermore, there are almost no
plans to reach them.

Nevertheless, there are many indications
that these forgotten people will be receptive
to the Gospel if the means and strategies are
developed to reach them. The new U.S. Center
for World Mission in Pasadena is small in comparison to the immensity of the task, but it is the
largest single property in the world today
dedicated exclusively to reaching the hidden
people. What has been launched in Pasadena
must alert us, as did that first satellite, that
we have entered a new age, and nothing short
of a total effort will conquer this last frontier.

AN OVERVIEW
FOR SUPER-BUSY PEOPLE

by Ralph D. Winter

The U.S. Center for World Mission is a group of former missionaries and mission leaders who in September 1978 took over an entire college campus in Pasadena, California, which was vacated by a Christian college that had moved to another city.

Already 110 people are working in the Center each day, performing a variety of functions, all of which focus on the development of new efforts to get the cause of frontier missions moving again in America. The exclusive emphasis is upon 16,750 populations around the world which are still beyond the reach of any existing church or mission. (We have dubbed these people "the hidden people.")

The cost of the entire project, **making it a self-sustaining venture which will no longer require donations,** is $15 million.

But, the Evangelical Movement in America today is bursting out all over with breathtaking new projects. Most of these seem to encompass the whole world in their purpose. Almost everyone knows Billy Graham, Jim Bakker, Robert Schuller, Pat Robertson, Bill Bright, Oral Roberts, Jerry Falwell, Morris Cerillo, etc. Just these eight brothers-in-Christ alone are out to raise $1500 million dollars. (That's 1.5 billion dollars.) By what audacity do WE propose to raise another $15 million, which amounts to an additonal 1 percent?

Well put! We are not famous like those men We have no radio or television program, no audience, no constituency, no mailing list of on-going donors, no millionaire friends.

WHO ARE WE, ANYHOW? IS THERE REALLY ANY DIFFERENCE IN WHAT WE'RE TRYING TO DO?

First of all, we are not going to be critical of these well-known leaders. I who write this am personally known to most of them, and I have great respect and admiration for all of them. I pray earnestly that God will bless their efforts.

The difference is we belong very nearly in a different world. First of all, I myself am a former missionary - commissioned in 1956. I worked for ten years with aboriginal peoples in Guatemala. I worked another ten years in a School of World Mission where a thousand missionaries from 90 countries passed through my classes. Yes, on the **Board of Reference** of the U.S. Center for World Mission we have eight well-known Christian leaders who are not necessarily mission leaders. But we have 42 **Consultants** who are virtually all specialists in missions, only a few known widely to the general public, but all very well-known in the world of missions. Our **Board of Directors** consists of nine missionaries or mission leaders plus three mission-devoted businessmen.

Furthermore, most of our friends and closest associates live and move and have their being in the world of missions.

I refer to the executives of the Interdenominational Foreign Mission Association and the Evangelical Foreign Missions Association, leaders of the major mission boards today (like Wycliffe Bible Translators, the Southern Baptist Foreign Board of Missions, Overseas Missionary Fellowship, Sudan Interior Mission, and various denominational boards of missions - Methodist, Presbyterian, American Baptist, Conservative Baptist, etc.). These are the people who know us well.

True, Pat Boone has been very kind to us. Billy Graham has gone out of his way. But it is a former missionary, Donald Hoke, founding director of the Billy Graham Center, who said, "This is the single most strategic institution in the world today aimed at evangelizing the 2 billion persons who can only be reached by "missionary" evangelism. You may freely use my name in commending the Center to God's people everywhere." Jim Montgomery, Overseas Field Director of Overseas Crusades said," If the U.S. Center for World Mission fails, our mission cannot succeed." Missionary families number among the most sacrificial supporters of this project.

Why? Because this, I believe, is **the first time a group of missionaries have themselves taken the initiative to establish a center in the U.S. which will study, evaluate, and assit all mission effort in a constructive and helpful way,** to move dynamically and decisively to push back the barriers limiting present efforts and penetrate the last 16,750 human groupings within which there is not yet a culturally relevant church.

AREN'T MISSIONS ALREADY DOING THIS?

Without any criticism intended, the answer is mainly "no"! Generally speaking, affluent Americans, far better able to contribute to overseas effort than ever in history are going home before the party is over - like a doctor leaving the delivery room before the baby is born. The mission agencies know full well there is an immense amount of work to be done, but the agencies are having a tough time keeping present work supported without adding new fields of endeavor. We want to help Americans rub their eyes, awake to the remaining challenge, not to be weary in well-doing, and give a massive new push to the cause of missions to the frontiers. We have no desire to add one more mission to compete with what is now being done.

AREN'T YOU PERHAPS OVER-EMPHASIZING "THE UNFINISHED TASK"?

Study the chart on the opposite page. Notice that column 5 represents the basic widely published statistics which add up to the total world's population of 4,321 million people (as of July 1, 1979). To the left of column 5 are four columns that break down those column 5 totals into two kinds of Christians and two kinds of non-Christians. It is column 4 on which the U.S. Center for World Mission and its sister Centers around the world are focused. You will note from the total of column 4 that it represents more than one-half of the world's population and 80 percent of the non-Christians of the world. Thus, column 4 is not only a larger task, but it is much more difficult than the column 3 task. The masses in column 3 are not only smaller in number but easier to reach: within every group listed in column 3 there are already at least some Christians in a worshipping fellowship that speaks their languages and represents their same cultures. This is precisely not true for column 4. In view of the truly staggering magnitude and complexity (see col. 7, 8, 9) of the column 4 task, one modest-sized campus devoted exclusively to it does not seem to be an over-emphasis!

WHAT DID YOU SAY ABOUT SISTER CENTERS?

We are not presuming for a moment that Americans will be or should be the only answer to the unfinished task of missions. It is a wonderful fact that we can confidently assume that Christians in every land are as willing as we are to try to fulfill the Great Commission. Therefore we assume

CHRISTIANS		NON-CHRISTIANS	
230	1,031 million (E-0)	604 million (E-1)	2,456 million (E-2 and E-3)
			The "Hidden People"

WORLD STATISTICS, MID-1979 IN MISSIONARY PERSPECTIVE
(population given in millions)

	1	2	3	4	5	6	7	8	9
	CHRISTIAN		NON-CHRISTIAN		POP.* TOTALS	N.A. FOREIGN MISSIONARIES		DIVERSITY IN COLUMN 4	
	Commit-ted	Nominal E-0	within range E-1	beyond E-2, E-3		working with 1,2,3	working with 4	langua-ges	sub-groups
WESTERN WORLD									
USA, CANADA	69	146	17	12	244	-		80	300
EUROPE, LAT. AM. N.Z., AUSTRALIA	60	719	187	151	1,117	15,018	1,000	480	950
SUB-TOTAL	129	865	204	163	1,361				
NON-WESTERN WLD									
CHINESE	2	1	140	737	880	1,217	100	50	2,000
HINDUS	6	11	40	506	563	950	50	200	3,000
MUSLIMS, ASIA**	.11	.05	20	493	513	100	50	300	3,500
MUSLIMS AFRICA	-	-	-	176	176	-	50	280	500
OTHER ASIANS	44	64	157	282	547	7,077	1,600	2,500	4,000
OTHER AFRICANS	49	90	43	99	251	9,338	500	1,500	2,500
SUB-TOTAL	101	166	400	2,293	2,960	33,700	3,350	5,390	16,750
	230	1,031	604	2,456	4,321				
	1,261 29%		604 20%	2,456 80%		91%	9%		
			3,960 71%			37,050			

* Population Reference Bureau, Washington, D.C.
** Note there are additional 26 million Muslims in the Western World

U.S. Center for World Mission
May, 1979

that the idea of a Center focused on frontier missions will be acceptable for every country (and for every region in large countries, like India). There are already boards of directors in South Africa, Scotland, South India, Singapore, Hong Kong and Korea concerned to establish sister centers. Interest exists in a half-dozen other countries. All these centers will be supported and operated by citizens of the respective countries. It is not for Americans to go around the world telling others what to do. We are delighted, however, whenever word of our efforts has aroused interest in doing the same thing, whether it is Brazil, Nigeria, etc. Our International Consultant, George W. Peters, has the responsibility of lending encouragement and maintaining contact with all such parallel interests in other lands. Only in this way can the job ever be properly done. All the Christians of the world must get involved!

CAN'T THE NATIONAL CHURCHES OVERSEAS DO THIS JOB BY THEMSELVES?

Many American Christians assume that somehow the job will be easier for, and more effectively done by, "national Christians." Where the job is a column 3 task (reaching out to people in the same culture and language as those national Christians) that is a true assumption. But the column 4 task is by definition as much a missionary task for so-called "national Christians" as it is for Americans. We are all "national Christians," meaning we are all citizens somewhere. But whoever we are we will have to learn a foreign language and adjust to a strange culture to reach column 4 people - column 9 shows that they live in at least 16,750 sub-groups where there is no church at all.

Furthermore, to expect the national churches to automatically be a success at this kind of missions is the same as assuming that an Anglo church in any American city can automatically be effective in reaching out to Navajos, Lebanese refugees, Chinese, or even Spanish-speaking people in their neighborhoods. No matter how much the church may want to evangelize these people, it is simply not the best instrument for the cross-cultural ministry which such a task involves. This requires special skills and special gifts. And throughout history it has required special organizations, supported by the church, but free to determine with missionary wisdom just how to do the job.

In the last twenty-five years many such "special organizations" have sprung up overseas. It is welcome news that Christians in other lands are responding to the call to get involved in missions which are also "foreign" to them. But the task is so immense that it is going to take a concerted effort on the part of Christians everywhere to fulfill Christ's command. We cannot escape our responsibility just because Christians elsewhere are beginning to help us bear the task.

WHY DO YOU NEED A CAMPUS?

We feel we must attack the root of the problem. Young people by the thousands streaming to Urbana and making a missionary decision do not have the hard facts upon which to build the serious next steps that can take them into a challenging task within the Great Commission.

Most of our campus at any given time will be filled with students taking a single semester out of their regular college course. Most will be from secular universities and colleges - because that is where 90 percent of all evangelical students are!

This special short course in "International Studies" has been developed over six years, three years on the Wheaton campus, and has had outstanding success in giving college young people a completely new foundation upon which to build their careers, whether or not they go overseas. They come away knowing not only what the Bible teaches about mission strategy but what 37,000 American missionaries are actually doing around the world, where they are concentrated, what agencies they work for, what languages and cultures they have or have not penetrated, what is left to be done and how to do it. It is called "International Studies" merely to safeguard the transfer of units to a secular school. But it amounts to a completely new Christian intellectual foundation for most students. Every church needs at least one member who has received this kind of intensive education in the worldwide Christian cause. Yet there is no secular university in the country that provides courses of this sort.

DO YOU HAVE A GRADUATE PROGRAM?

Yes. We aready have a sister corporation (under the very same Board of Directors) called the William Carey International University. The state of California has authorized us to grant six M.A. degrees and five Ph.D. degrees, in fields such as Chinese Studies, Hindu Studies, Muslim Studies, Tribal Studies and International Development. In addition to our very special one-semester program aiready mentioned, we expect to have a growing force of experts on campus connected with a series of mission strategy offices dealing in specific detail with the great unwon blocks of humanity. These senior researchers will mainly be missionaries retired, returned, reassigned to us, who will bring immense field experience and constitute an outstanding graduate faculty. Furthermore, there are at least 300 U.S. missionaries scattered all over the globe who have Ph. D. degrees. The word "International" in the title of the university corporation indicates our intention to set up adjunct faculty and graduate committees in most of the major centers in the non-Western World and thus be prepared to sponsor both missionaries and nationals in graduate degree studies without their having to come to the U.S. This will also - and most importantly - allow us to harvest hundreds of thousands of hours of additional field research at essentially no cost of us.

WHY THIS PARTICULAR CAMPUS IN PASADENA?

First of all **the place.** In the last 25 years Southern California has become the one place on the entire earth's surface most closely approximating a **Pentecost of Nations.** There are larger concentrations of a larger number of nationalities there than anywhere else in the world (and generally each foreign group has a higher percentage of

Christians than in its home country!). This fact has implications both for training programs and stategic developments. Secondly, **this campus.** This was and is literally the only campus available, where we can set up shop, start operating and claim the ground for this dream. Despite the active competition of a monied spiritual cult that had a temporary lease on 2/3 of the campus, we now own it having completed the down payment in September of 1978. To build the same campus elsewhere would cost almost three times as much. To lose this campus by failing to make the payments will set back the exclusive and crucially necessary emphasis of this Center for many years - at a time when to delay is truly tragic in terms of world events.

IN A PRACTICAL SENSE, HOW DO YOU EXPECT TO PAY FOR THIS CAMPUS?

We are already being carried on a wave of positive response. All kinds of leaders of all kinds ranging from devout but hard-headed businessmen to mission statesmen have investigated our methods and objectives. No one, no church, has heard us out and turned us down.

While we lack the widespread notoriety that would make it easy, we feel sure that as fast as people hear about the challenge they will respond.

Obviously we are making it harder for ourselves by asking for only a $15 one-time gift, but there are two good reasons for this: we do not wish in any way to conflict with regular mission agencies, and we do indeed want to get to as many people as possible with this challenge.

One challenging plan is for people who want to help us to organize letter-writing parties to send out a specially prepared letter to their friends. If just 50 people sent out an average of 30 letters each, this would bring back 1,000 of the $15.00 one-time donations we seek, assuming only 2/3 of the friends responded.

We would much prefer that to big donations, and we are eager to help arouse Americans to give more for frontier missions through standard mission agencies of all kinds.

YOU HAVE TOLD US ABOUT EVERYTHING AND EVERYONE EXCEPT YOURSELF! WHAT IS YOUR BACKGROUND?

I was born in California, grew up in Christian Endeavor, Youth for Christ, Navigators (in the Navy in WW II), graduated from Cal Tech, taught one year at Westmont College, attended the first "Urbana" (at Toronto), helped launch a non-professional missionary effort to Afghanistan; further studies at various places (including Prairie Bible Institute) led to an M.A. in Education at Columbia University, a Ph.D. at Cornell in Anthropology and Linguistics and later a B.D. at Princeton. I worked with Mayan Indians in Guatemala for ten years, helped to found the theological-education-by-extension movement (extending seminary to Indians), was elected Executive Secretary of the Latin American Association of Theological Schools, Northern Region (17 countries), was invited to join McGavran and Tippett in the second year of the new Fuller School of World Mission in 1967. In 1972 I helped to found the American Society of Missiology (of which I have been both Secretary and President), the William Carey Library, the Summer Institute of International Studies, the Order for World Evangelization, etc. I was asked to give a plenary address at the Lausanne International Congress on World Evangelization, and the opening address at the 1976 Triennial Mission Executives' retreat of the Interdenominational Foreign Mission Association and the Evangelical Foreign Missions Association, the same thing again at the opening session of the 1979 EFMA Executive Retreat. My father has been an active lay Christian, headed up the development of the freeway system for the City of Los Angeles. My older brother, an engineer, has been President of the Board of African Enterprise, and my younger brother is President of Westmont College. On November 1st, 1976 when I left Fuller Seminary I was a tenured full Professor of the Historic Development of the Christian Movement.

WHAT IS YOUR THEOLOGY?

Our people are central in the evangelical movement. We adhere without qualification to the full inspiration and authority of the Bible, to the uniqueness and saving work of Christ, to the power of the Holy Spirit and His guidance in our lives. Specifically we hold the Lausanne Covenant and the statements of faith of the Interdenominational Foreign Mission Association (IFMA) and the Evangelical Foreign Missions Association (EFMA) as bench mark documents with which participating individuals and organizations must be in agreement. We do not have nor do we contemplate any formal relationship with any denomination or church council, but we do welcome representatives of evangelical mission agencies to work with us in our various strategy institutes and mobilization centers. All of our staff are supported by some mission agency or other and are on loan on a short or long-term basis to us except for several of our central staff who raise their own support directly under the banner of the U.S. Center for World Mission.

Dear Friend of the U.S. Center for World Mission,

We have always been absolutely straightforward with you.

As we now face our last really large quarterly payment, September 15th, we are just as hopeless, humanly speaking, as we have been prior to the first two major deadlines, needing 44,000 more $15.95 donations in order to meet the $660,000 required. Although we are now legal owners of the campus, having completed the full down payment of $1.5 million last September, nevertheless if we fail to make this payment, we will in fact not only lose the property but the entire down payment as well. If we make that last large quarterly payment, we will still have $175,000 per quarter to pay. But by then we'll likely have enough grass roots momentum to carry on.

God may choose to do miracles for us, as He has in the past. But we feel He has asked us in any case to be dead serious about sharing the knowledge of the world's Hidden Peoples with a million American evangelicals. And there is no more sure, more economical way to pay for this campus than to know that thousands of small donors are passing the challenge on to eventually a million people. This will not only secure the campus and found the Center, but will give new vision to a million people--an equally essential accomplishment.

This does not mean we will not accept larger donations. And we have! It means we do not ask for more than a "vote"--a one-time small gift of $15.95. The fascinating and significant reasons for this unusual policy are spelled out in the next few pages.

We hope this small book will constitute a great and grave challenge to your heart and your schedule during the next few weeks. Who will suffer if you just lay this aside and do nothing? The Hidden People, whose plight is outside your normal round of activities. A lot hangs on your personal response.

Yours in His Commission,

Ralph D. Winter

Ralph D. Winter

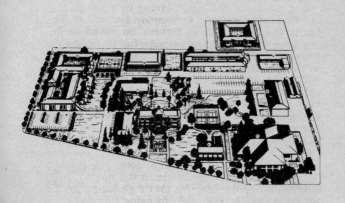

WILL YOU CAMPAIGN FOR THE HIDDEN PEOPLE?

FASCINATING AND SIGNIFICANT REASONS FOR OUR UNUSUAL $15 GRAPEVINE APPROACH

1) Knowing we'll never ask people for a second gift, more churches will cooperate. It may actually be easier to get more money by asking for less.
2) Meanwhile, with more churches cooperating, more people will gain a vision of the Hidden Peoples and begin to give new and additional money to the frontier mission activities of all the normal mission agencies.
3) Mission agencies will not sense competition but reinforcement. We'll not be winning away their steady supporters but adding thousands of new ones. The effect will be a missionary "broadening of the base" of mission giving in America.
4) Our approach does not employ fund raisers or high cost direct mail methods but simply relies upon the amazing and wonderful grapevine of personal recommendations. This is the method by which the gospel has spread since the first century. There is no more economical means.

OUR OBJECTIVES IN CONCRETE TERMS

1) Along with many others, our goal is "a church for every people by the year 2000."
2) By 1984, therefore, we feel that every one of the 16,750 Hidden Peoples must be known and accounted for in the plan of some evangelical mission agency somewhere in the world.
3) To do this we need by 1984 a global network of 60 sister centers, each focusing their own national resources on the unfinished task.
4) To do this, present U.S. mission agencies will still be required to play a large role and must have new resources of people and funds.
5) Within 3 years we seek to capture the imagination and backing of 1,000,000 Americans for a new interest and commitment to Frontier Missions through their own churches.

6) To do that we need to undergird the $15 million Funding Budget of the U.S. Center for World Mission by a million founding gifts of $15.95 each.

7) To do that we need to meet the "last large quarterly payment" (See p. 7) lest we lose the very base we stand upon.

8) To do that we need to get "the vote" of 44,000 people by September 15th as $15.95 Founders of the U.S. Center for World Mission.

9) To do that we need you, dear Founder, to help us share the challenge as described below in the way only you can do.

THE STEPS YOU CAN TAKE

Many individuals and churches across our country have already participated in this movement. They have responded in two significant ways:

1) <u>They have "cast their vote" for the Hidden People.</u>
   a) The "Founder" is an individual who gives $15.95 as their one and only contribution to the founding budget of the USCWM.
   b) The "Founding Church" is a church whose pastor and/or missions leadership have chosen to share this vision and concern with their congregation, allowing each member the opportunity to "cast their vote".

2) <u>They have joined the campaign and encouraged others to "cast their vote".</u>
   a) The "Campaigner" is an individual who has chosen to believe God for at least three other people with whom they can share this vision.
   b) The "Campaigning Church" is a congregation whose membership has chosen to reach out wherever they can, believing God that they can reach at least three other churches with this vision.

We have seen some individuals not only reach out to their friends, but the word has passed from those friends to a third and fourth generation. The grapevine is spreading this vision! We believe it is very possible one person could be responsible for reaching 1000 people before the grapevine has ended.

May we recommend 6 steps that might help you discover your potential contribution to spreading this
vision?

1) Pray for the Hidden People. Join with others
   around you in praying for the final push to reach
   these 16,750 Hidden Peoples. We can send you a
   prayer sheet which will help you to do this.

2) Determine your spheres of influence. Each of us
   has many circles of friends. We interact with
   small groups (Bible studies, committees, prayer
   cells) as well as large groups (churches, Sunday
   school classes, Christian organizations). For
   those who have traveled, deep relationships might
   exist in three or four areas of the country. What
   is your field of relationships? How many could
   you reach with this word? Spend some time and
   pray about those with whom God might be asking
   you to share this concern.

3) Decide how best to share this vision. Let us share
   with you some simple and effective ways to spread
   this vision:

   a) The "Grapevine" letter. Hundreds of people
      have been reached with the push toward the
      Hidden People as a result of receiving this
      specially designed letter which can be passed
      to others through the mail.

   b) "Evening with a Purpose". The General Direc-
      tor, Dr. Winter, will be spending time in the
      homes of people across the country in the next
      months. But a specially dedigned slide-tape
      presentation will be sent to you allowing anyone
      to invite people into their homes to hear the
      concerns of the USCWM. Some have found this
      a more intimate way to share the vision with
      their friends.

   c) "Loan the book "Once More Around Jericho".
      People don't find the time to read a book which
      has been given to them. But by loaning it,
      people will need to read it before they give it
      back to you. Try loaning your book!

   d) Hold a "Hidden People" Sunday. Church leader-
      ship can decide to have one Sunday when they
      can give each and everyone in their congrega-
      tion the opportunity to "cast their vote" for the
      Hidden People. There is an 18-minute film as

well as bulletin inserts available which will communicate this vision effectively. We have a special Pastor's Kit which you can give to the leadership in your church.

Feel free to discover other creative ways to spread this vision through the materials we offer.

4) Don't do it alone. Set the example for others who wish to do the same as you. This will multiply the number of people who will be impacted with this vision because of sharing your concern. You might also coordinate materials for your area so that "campaigners" and "campaigning churches" will have ready access to materials.

5) Make a "faith promise" of people. Set some goals. How many Founders are you willing to believe God for? (Remember: think second, third, and fourth generations!) Maybe you can reach one person every week between now and September 15th. How many will you trust God for over the next year?

6) Keep informed. The monthly bulletin Mission Frontiers will give you a vital update on the USCWM developments. Let's stay in touch---report in and let us know what you are doing and how God seems to be using you in your area. We want to communicate regularly to those involved in this campaign. People, events and opportunities are news we want to share with those involved in the campaign.

Any questions? Call or write to:

Brad Gill
Mission Mobilization
(213) 794-7155

YES! I'LL HELP IN THIS EMERGENCY!

☐ I'd like to know more about what is involved in being a Coordinator, so I can share the challenge with 1,000 people. (*You may wish to phone us: 213-794-7155*).

☐ I'd like to be a Campaigner. Please send me _____ copies of the specially prepared letter.

☐ I have not yet sent in my own $15.95 tax deductible gift. Please find it enclosed. Please send me a free copy of this book.

☐ I have shared this with others already. Here are _____ checks for $15.95 which I am sending in for the people I have contacted. Please send them this book.

☐ Tell me how my church or group can see the film *"Penetrating the Last Frontiers"*.

NAME _____ PHONE _____

ADDRESS _____ ZIP _____

Mail to U.S.C.W.M., 1605 Elizabeth St., Pasadena, CA 91104 (213) 794-7155